One
Flesh

McDougal & Associates
Servants of Christ and Stewards of the
Mysteries of God

One Flesh

Discovering Kingdom Principles
for Your Marriage

by

Jane P. McCoy

Published by:

McDougal & Associates
18896 Greenwell Springs Road
Greenwell Springs, LA 70739

www.ThePublishedWord.com

McDougal & Associates is an organization dedicated to the spreading of the Gospel of the Lord Jesus Christ to as many people as possible in the shortest time possible.

ISBN: 978-1-950398-10-2

Printed in the U.S., the U.K. and Australia
For Worldwide Distribution

Dedication

To my late parents—**Odelia Davis Perrault and Wilfred Perrault, Sr.**—I dedicate this work. You would be proud to know that I have excelled, just as you declared over my life. I wish you were here to celebrate with me. Missing you both.

Love always
Jane

My Desire

My desire for every married couple and every single person, both male and female, is that you gain valuable insight from this book. This is a magnificent model or resource guide to follow, whether you are married or preparing for marriage. My hope is that, working with this book, you will develop a spiritual awareness, not only of yourself, but also of the person you desire to spend the rest of your life with.

Contents

> *Prepare your work outside*
> *And get it ready for yourself in the field;*
> *Afterward build your house*
> *and establish a home.*
> Proverbs 24:27, AMP

We are commanded by God to prepare for what's ahead; preparing requires purpose, planning and practice. Preparing for a life journey with another person takes love, endurance, commitment, a sense of wholeness, completeness and assurance.

Getting to know yourself and the person you will invest in is the first step toward building your marriage, but start building your marriage before your wedding day. A wedding day is filled with memories, but a marriage never remains the same, because you will be forever building something new together.

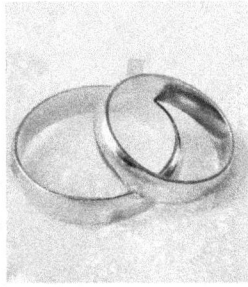

Introduction

When we hear of someone preparing for marriage, we get so excited in the planning of that big day—the wedding. The bride-to-be invests many hours to ensure that her wedding day is one which all will remember. She will set a large budget to guarantee that everything she ever dreamed her wedding to be will be fulfilled. She carefully chooses everything—from her bridesmaids, floral arrangements, the menu, the music and the seating arrangements, down to the very linen napkins. Her dress, hair, shoes and makeup must be perfect. Colors must all be well coordinated. With much excitement, the focus is on "the Big Day."

To receive a marriage proposal from the love of your life is the dream of most women: MY WEDDING DAY. This *is* a special day, and it *is* advisable to spend time preparing for it. However, I believe it is equally important to invest ample time getting to know the person you will be committing to, the one you will be spending the rest of your life with. We should spend much more time preparing for the marriage itself, since it is a lifetime commitment.

Tragically, most people spend lots of time preparing for the *wedding* and very little time planning for the *marriage* itself. Again, marriage is a lifelong commitment, a vow taken before God and before many witnesses. You want nothing less than a perfect wedding day, filled with compliments and memories, a day that will be cherished forever — as long as you both shall live. But you also want a great marriage.

Because of the lack of planning for the actual marriage and because many don't understand the roles each partner should play, this leaves the door open to the enemy to wreak havoc on the marriage. The result is severe damage to the home and, ultimately, to the personal lives of the man and woman involved. Memories of that day then become wrapped in disappointment, grief, bitterness and anguish, and in far too many cases, an inability to forgive. The end result is devastation.

Marriage teaches us how to love. It teaches us how to share. It teaches us how to respect each other. Marriage is not textbook magic; it is a willingness to share life with another, in good times and bad, in

Introduction

lack and in plenty alike. Marriage teaches us to be selfless, compassionate, loyal and generous.

I believe the first important thing when contemplating marriage is having a knowledge of covenantal precepts, what they mean and how to fulfill their obligations. God instituted marriage after the Edenic covenant. He has been about covenant relationships from the day of Creation in Genesis 2:16:

And the LORD God commanded the man, saying, Of every tree of the garden thou mayest freely eat:

The first, or Edenic Covenant, required the following responsibilities of Adam:
1. To propagate the race;
2. To subdue the earth for man;
3. To have dominion over the animal creation;
4. To care for the garden and eat its fruits and herbs; and
5. To abstain from eating of one tree, the tree of the knowledge of good and evil, on penalty of death for disobedience.

The Edenic covenant is one of several covenants mentioned in the Old Testament. Others include the Adamic, the Noahic and Abrahamic covenants, just to mention a few. In the Abrahamic covenant, during the Dispensation of Promise, God made an agreement with Abraham, the father of our faith (see Genesis 18:19). God chose Abraham because he understood the principles of covenant relationship, and God trusted that he would teach his children and grandchildren after him to walk in the ways of the Lord:

> *For I know him, that he will command his children and his household after him, and they shall keep the way of the LORD, to do justice and judgment; that the LORD may bring upon Abraham that which he hath spoken of him.*
>
> Genesis 18:19

It is my belief that covenant relationship begins long before the special day, the actual wedding day. I believe we ought to live a life of covenant principles within our homes and everywhere we go on a daily basis.

Covenant relationship starts at infancy. God expects parents to train up a child in the way he should go, train that child to live within covenant guidelines. When we are trained from infancy in

Introduction

these principles, both our childhood and adulthood will experience less crises of relationships.

A relationship is one of the most important elements of any covenant. Therefore, if we were trained in lifelong covenant relationship building, then entering into a marriage covenant would not be something as monumental as it is for far too many today. If we were trained to walk in the way of the Lord, covenant would be second nature to us.

> *Train up a child in the way he should go: and when he is old, he will not depart from it.*
>
> Proverbs 22:6

God has pressed upon my heart to share with others—both men and women—some of the most crucial steps for both the married and those preparing for marriage. I pray that this study will be an enrichment to your soul, that you would be empowered to effectively prepare for this new covenant relationship. May this study help you prepare to build a solid marriage that will last for many years.

In this study, you will gain wisdom and insight to know what to ask and what to look for before you say, "I do." After you have gone through this book, hopefully with spiritual guidance, you will have more confidence, knowing that you have gained valuable tools and spiritual insight that will enable you to walk victoriously into your marriage in Jesus' name and for His glory.

This study can be done in a group setting with both parties present. However, it should be approached as a personalized quest to prepare for marriage. I recommend that you have a mature spiritual leader to assist you with questions and to give you clarity as needed. The advice they give you should be scripturally based.

You will notice that the entirety of this study is scripturally based. It is recommended that you follow through with your own Bible, not just reading a verse here and there, but reading and, if necessary, reviewing whole passages related to marriage. You should also keep handy a pen and paper to answer the study questions at the end of each section. Additionally, you will want to note any areas of concern you wish to discuss with your spiritual guide and/or with your marriage partner. Do not go on until each concern is resolved.

It is also advisable to complete my book *Breaking Free: A Manual for Finding Deliverance through Prayer and Fasting.*[1] Remember, you are doing all of this as an investment into your marriage.

1. (Greenwell Springs, Louisiana, McDougal & Associates:2019)

Introduction

After completing these exercises, you should be well equipped to recognize your duties and to function as a spouse should according to the Scriptures. When we know what is expected of us and have the understanding to carry out these expectations, it makes it so much easier to accept the responsibilities that come with our marital duties.

Since God instituted marriage, it must become habit that we always put Him first. Making Him the center of the marriage will ensure victory when trials come. There will inevitably be some ups and downs along the way (see Deuteronomy 11:1 and 13-14).

The Bible cautions us against the sins of fornication and adultery. The simplest way to avoid these sins is to have your own marriage partner. God said:

> *Nevertheless, to avoid fornication, let every man have his own wife, and let every woman have her own husband.*   1 Corinthians 7:2

So marriage is a wise step to take. However, we must always enter into marriage with the right motives and in God's way.

Be blessed now as you study *One Flesh: Discovering Kingdom Principles for your Marriage.*

Jane P. McCoy

CHAPTER 1

What the Bible Says about Marriage

Marriage is honourable in all, and the bed un-defiled: but whoremongers and adulterers God will judge. Hebrews 13:4

Let's begin with some definitions, so that we are on the same page:

Marriage means "the state of being united to a person of the opposite sex as husband or wife in a consensual and contractual relationship recognized by law."

Consensual means "existing or made by mutual consent without an act of writing: involving or based on mutual consent."

Contractual means "relating to or constituting a contract."

Contract means "to give an account of; to show or establish logical or causal connection between."[2]

There are three elements of a contract or covenant:
1. **Promises**: what you will receive from the covenant
2. **Agreements**: what is expected from you out of the covenant
3. **Conditions**: what you must do in order to receive full benefit from the covenant.

Just as marriage is a covenant with these three aspects, so your walk with God is a covenant with the same three important concepts.

1. The Promises

On their wedding day, a couple repeats a series of vows to publicly affirm their lifelong commitment to one another. These vows are made before a minister, before people and before God.

---

2. Merriam-Webster Dictionary

2. The Agreement

After the vows are repeated, the minister asks, "Do you … ?" and the man and woman respond with the words, "I do." Those are strong English words to affirm an agreement. Once the couple agrees to the promises, then the marriage covenant is legally sealed in the eyes of God and the witnesses.

3. The Conditions

While love should be unconditional, the marriage vows come with spiritual conditions. The condition is faithfulness to your marriage partner. You must now do as you have promised.

The first marriage in the Bible took place in the Garden of Eden when God brought the woman (Eve) to the man (Adam). The man must be prepared to take on the role of a husband, according to the Creator's divine order. So, let's look at how God prepared Adam for his help meet.

God and Adam had a relationship. We know this because they communed with each other. Adam recognized the voice of God. God had a purpose for Adam, and it was to till the ground and maintain the garden which was in Eden. So, Adam had responsibilities, and he was accountable to God.

Adam was very intelligent because God trusted him to name the fowls of the air and every beast that was created:

> *And out of the ground the LORD God formed every beast of the field, and every fowl of the air; and brought them unto Adam to see what he would call them: and whatsoever Adam called every living creature, that was the name thereof.*
>
> Genesis 2:19

There are three things we see God working out in Adam before giving him the larger responsibility of having a wife and children. First, Adam had to have a relationship with God. Second, God gave Adam a job and responsibilities. He worked and had dominion over the things he named. Adam understood his purpose. Third, Adam used his intellect to name all the cattle, beasts and fowls of the air and, most importantly, he even named Eve, his wife, and understood that she had been made a part of who he was. He understood that Eve was taken out of him and, therefore, was a part of him.

What the Bible Says about Marriage

God entrusted Adam with what He gave him to do, and Adam understood the importance of working with God. Through this example, we see that a man is not prepared to take on a help meet unless these several characteristics are met.

In Genesis 2, after Creation, for the very first time, God said that something was *"not good."* What was it that was *"not good"*? It was the fact that Adam was alone. It was *"not good,"* God said, that this man should be alone:

> *And the LORD God said, It is not good that the man should be alone; I will make him an help meet for him.*   Genesis 2:18

Adam was incomplete without his wife, and God wanted to make Adam complete. Adam was surrounded by the animals God had created, but none of them was like him. None of them could complete him:

> *And Adam gave names to all cattle, and to the fowl of the air and to every beast of the field; but for Adam there was not found an help meet for him. And the LORD God caused a deep sleep to fall upon Adam and he slept: and he took one of*

One Flesh

his ribs, and closed up the flesh instead thereof;
and the rib, which the LORD *God had taken from*
man, made he a woman, and brought her unto
the man. And Adam said, this is now bone of my
bones, and flesh of my flesh: she shall be called
Woman, because she was taken out of Man.
Therefore, shall a man leave his father and his
mother, and shall cleave unto his wife: and they
shall be one flesh.   Genesis 2:20-24

The New Testament has many teachings on marriage. Here are some relevant verses that show the seriousness and the legally and morally binding quality of marriage:

Wherefore they are no more twain, but one flesh.
What therefore God hath joined together, let not
man put asunder.   Matthew 19:6

For this cause shall a man leave his father and
mother, and shall be joined unto his wife, and
they two shall be one flesh.   Ephesians 5:31

For the woman which hath an husband is bound
by the law to her husband so long as he liveth;
but if the husband be dead, she is loosed from
the law of her husband.   Romans 7:2

What the Bible Says about Marriage

And unto the married I command, yet not I, but the Lord, let not the wife depart from her husband. But and if she departs, let her remain unmarried, or be reconciled to her husband: and let not the husband put away his wife.

1 Corinthians 7:10-11

Those who take marriage vows are under solemn obligation and are legally and morally bound before God to their spouse in marriage.

God commends marriage:

Whoso findeth a wife findeth a good thing, and obtaineth favour of the LORD.

Proverbs 18:22

A man finds his help meet and also finds favor with God. The two are linked. This leads me to say that since marriage originated with God and is recommended by God, there is no place in marriage for abuse. God is not an abuser, and He does not give us permission to abuse others. I firmly believe that God does not condone abuse of any kind.

Now, let us visit this unusual term *help meet*:

And Adam gave names to all cattle, and to the fowl of the air, and to every beast of the field;

One Flesh

*but for Adam there was not found an help meet
for him.*   Genesis 2:20

The Hebrew phrase used here that is translated
into English as *"help meet,"* according to *Strong's*
is "H5826; *ezer* (ay'-zer) meaning aid; help comes
from the Hebrew word *'azar* (aw-zas') meeting to
surround, protect or aid; help, succor."

The wife is one who will protect her husband
without limits. In today's society, many believe
that the wife is a person who always stays at home,
caring for children and the household. From what
we can tell thus far, God's intent for the wife was to
be of much more service than that to her husband.

Meeting to surround means "to make complete." A
wife is to protect her husband, whereas society con-
siders this duty to be strictly for the man. The wife
also will aid her husband with whatever support he
needs, be it emotional, psychological, spiritual or
physical. God never put a limit on what the "help
meet" should do to make her husband complete.

A husband works hard at his job, but he also has
the weight of the family's well-being on his shoul-
ders. This can and often does become very stressful.
The wife must be available to offer him support,
relief, prayers and encouragement. Although the

husband is to make available the house, the dwelling, the wife is the builder of the home, which includes her husband and children.

A wise woman builds her house with her bare hands. Therefore, a wife is much more than one who has babies. She is one who holds her home together. When we all are asleep, she is still up, making her rounds, ensuring that everyone is doing well and all are asleep. Only then will she lay her own head on the pillow. Then, many times during the night, she may be awake praying for her family.

A wife, therefore, must be a wise and a God-fearing woman who knows her worth and value, especially to her family. Such a woman is a gift from God:

> *Who can find a virtuous woman? for her price*
> *is far above rubies.*   Proverbs 31:10

A wise women wears many different hats. She is both nurse and doctor to her family. She is responsible with managing finances, making ends meet with whatever budget she is given to work with. She is the peacekeeper or mediator in the family, always loving, making peace, being patient, judging fairly and with understanding toward each member of her family. She is wise in her decision making, consulting with her husband and submitting to his advice. She is always diligent in business, never folding her hands. There are never enough hours in a day for her. The woman is the keeper of the home, a safe place.

Dealing with Premarital Sexual Relationships

According to webmd.com, a great majority of Americans have sex before marrying. Premarital sex research shows that such behavior is the norm in the U.S. and has been for the past fifty years. The latest study shows that by age 20, 75% of Americans have had premarital sex, and that number rises to 95% by age 44.[3]

I share these numbers with you so that you know how naïve some can be when it comes to believing that all are virgins (as they would have others to believe). What I want to discuss is the need to break the bonds of unhealthy or ungodly soul ties before you enter a covenant or contract with another.

One way a soul tie is formed is through sexual intercourse outside of marriage. A soul tie is an emotional bond that forms an attachment. These

3. https://www.webmd.com/sex-relationships/news/20061220/premarital-sex-the-norm-in-america

may be godly or ungodly, pure or wicked. Most people use the term *soul ties* to refer to connections linking people. However, most focus on the ungodly ties, those formed by and for ungodly reasons. For every ungodly soul tie, there must be repentance, and renunciation before you say, "I do."

The Scriptures say, *"What therefore God hath joined together, let no man put asunder"* (Matthew 19:6). This term *put asunder* means "to put space between or put apart."

Put asunder (G5563, *chorizo*) "to place room between, that is, part; reflexively to go away; depart, put asunder, separate."

Sex is an intimate act constructed by God for humankind to fulfill their marital contract obligations: to be fruitful, to multiply and to replenish the earth. Whenever two people come together in sexual intercourse outside of marriage, ungodly soul ties are formed, binding that person to all other persons their partner had sexual contact with. Fornication is sin and is an entrapment.

It is imperative to have a mature spiritual mentor to help guide you through the process of identifying the sexual sin and the persons involved in order to

One Flesh

break this ungodly intruder before you join yourself lawfully to another. For more details on ungodly soul ties and how to overcome them, please read my book, *Soul Ties, An Inside Look.*

Study Questions

1. Have you ever broken a contract? If so, why?

2. Do you believe a contract should be broken simply because one now feels the obligation is no longer necessary?

3. When should a contract be broken between married parties?

4. What does "help meet" mean to you?

5. In what ways can a wife be of help to her husband?

6. Should a career, family, ministry or any other external situation be a reason or reasons to end a contract? If so, why?

7. Have you and/or your spouse to be engaged in premarital sex? If so, have the resulting ungodly soul ties been broken?

8. Have all premarital affairs been thoroughly dealt with?

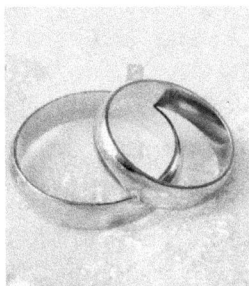

CHAPTER 2

One Flesh, Two Personalities

*This is a great mystery: but I speak concerning
Christ and the church.*   Ephesians 5:32

God created us human beings with boundaries.
The word *existence* comes from a word meaning
"to stand apart." Before there were two people in
the garden, there was one person, Adam. Adam
and Eve, then, each had an identity as a unique
human being apart from the other. Their identities
as separate individuals were crucial for their health
together. In the same way, God gives us boundaries, so we know where we end and others begin.
These boundaries include our own thoughts, feelings, hopes, dreams, fears, values and beliefs. These
things set us apart, reminding us of our separate-
ness as individuals. We must respect each other's
boundaries.

One Flesh

Now, let's address the matter of one flesh, but two personalities. Marriage mirrors the relationship of Christ and the Church, His Bride. When a man and a woman get married, they don't lose their individual identities. As a couple, they agree to participate in a relationship, but each of them continues to have his or her own life. Her life is not his life; nor is his life her life. They have become one union with a mission, and that requires them to do specific things for Christ's sake.

Marriages get in trouble when either spouse violates the other's space and boundaries. When they married, it didn't mean that there were no more individual rights. Each still has the right to free space, the right to free speech, the right to choose, the right to be treated with dignity and respect and the right to be free from abuse—be it emotional, psychological, physical or sexual. The difference in marriage is that the two have come together to do what only married people are required to do in the eyes of the Lord. For example, have children and raise them up into godly offspring and point them in the right direction (see Psalm 127).

In marriage, we must always recognize each other's feelings and desires and the limit of what can be sacrificed. Failing to do so produces an atmosphere of control, lack of respect, domination and abuse. Married people are responsible people, and they have the wellbeing of others in mind.

You may have heard a spouse say, "You are my life, my everything." That individual has not accepted their personal responsibilities. Why? Because they don't have a clue about who he or she is, and, therefore, that person cannot function in the position appointed by God. There will always be problems in a marriage when a spouse cannot define his or her mate as an individual. Knowing yourself is the beginning of setting healthy boundaries.

Marriage, like every other healthy relationship, requires boundaries. If you're not familiar with healthy boundaries, the marriage and your mate will suffer. Boundaries, when properly executed, become our safeguards.

God gave Adam a command before he was joined to his wife Eve. How Adam delivered that command to Eve the Scriptures do not tell us. God made it plain to Adam what he could freely do and what he could not do. Likewise, the Lord has set boundaries for all of us. They are His commandments, and they keep us safe and within His protective will.

One Flesh

God also told Adam what would happen if he did not obey, if he chose to trespass the boundaries set for him by the Creator. There were many trees in the garden, but there were two very special trees in the midst of the garden. One of them was the tree of life, and the other was the tree of the knowledge of good and evil:

> And the LORD God commanded the man, saying, Of every tree of the garden thou mayest freely eat: but of the tree of the knowledge of good and evil, thou shalt not eat of it: for in the day that thou eatest thereof thou shalt surely die. Genesis 2:16-17

One day, when Eve was alone in the garden, the serpent showed up, and they began to fellowship one with another. The serpent spoke to Eve, and she honored him with a response:

> Now the serpent was more subtle than any beast of the field which the LORD God had made. And he said unto the woman, Yea, hath God said, Ye shall not eat of every tree of the garden? And the woman said unto the serpent, We may eat of the fruit of the trees of the garden: but of the fruit of the tree which is in the midst of the garden, God

One Flesh, Two Personalities

hath said, Ye shall not eat of it, neither shall ye
touch it, lest ye die.   Genesis 3:1-3

Please note that Satan tempted Eve, not with the tree
of life, but with the tree of the knowledge of good and
evil. It would, he said, make her and Adam *"like God"*
(Verse 5). Eve responded to the serpent, acknowledg-
ing the fact that she knew about the trees, but adding
that God had warned them not to even touch this
particular tree or they would die.

God had not said that in His recorded command
to Adam. Had Adam told Eve about the trees and
that she should not touch this one? The Scriptures
don't say. Now, however, Eve was suddenly infatu-
ated with a tree that had the power to make them
"like God," and she was also suddenly unconcerned
about death—physical or spiritual.

Eve was spending way too much time with the serpent. The serpent was beginning to twist the Word
of God and to mix truth with lies. We know that a
half-truth is still a lie. But now Eve could not seem
to control herself. As the serpent lured her onward
with enticing thoughts, she moved ever closer to the
fateful tree:

And the serpent said unto the woman, ye shall
not surely die for God doth know that in the day

One Flesh

> *ye eat thereof, then your eyes shall be opened, and ye shall be as gods, knowing good and evil. And the woman saw that the tree was good for food, and that it was pleasant to the eyes, and a tree to be desired to make one wise, she took of the fruit thereof, and did eat, and gave also unto her husband with her; and he did eat. And the eyes of them both were opened, and they knew that they were naked.* Genesis 3:4-7

Looks can be deceiving. Everything that looks like gold is not true gold, and everything that looks good is not always good for us. Therefore, we must always look to the instructions of God, through His written Word, that we may live and be safe. His Word has declared:

> *Love not the world, neither the things that are in the world. If any man loves the world, the love of the Father is not in him. For all that is in the world, the lust of the flesh, and the lust of the eyes, and the pride of life, is not of the Father, but is of the world.* 1 John 2:15-16

Wherever there is an enticement to sin, one or more of these three lust will be present. Learn to flee from them:

One Flesh, Two Personalities

Therefore, let no man say when he is tempted, I am tempted of God: for God cannot be tempted with evil, neither tempted he any man. But every man is tempted, when he is drawn away of his own lust, and enticed. Then when lust hath conceived, it bringeth forth sin, when it is finished, bringeth forth death.

James 1:13-15

Eve was drawn in by her own lusts and desires. Satan justified her behavior by accusing God to her, making it look like He was a liar. *"Ye shall not surely die,"* he assured her. And the tragic thing is that Eve was listening and, worse, believing Satan's lie.

Everything was about to change for this couple, and not only for them, but also for all those who would be born on this earth afterward. They had once walked around with no clothing, for it was a time of innocence. Everything had been pure, and there was no knowledge of good and evil. But one bite of the forbidden fruit, and they had to run for cover. Ripping leaves from nearby fig trees, they tried to cover their guilt and shame.

Can you imagine how gratifying it was for the serpent to have caused mankind to fall from his perfect state? Man's willful disobedience to the commands of God brought sin and death upon the entire human race. Thank God for Jesus Christ, for in Him all those who believe can be made alive again:

> *For since by man came death, by man came also the resurrection of the dead. For as in Adam all die, even so in Christ shall all be made alive.*
>
> 1 Corinthians 15:21-23

Study Questions:

1. How important is effective communication?

2. How important is it to ask for clarification when you don't fully understand something?

3. What happens if we make assumptions?

4. What could you do to avoid being lured into disobeying a godly command?

5. How important is it to consider what you are thinking about?

6. Why did God forbid the first man and woman to eat of the tree of the knowledge of good and evil?

CHAPTER 3

Disobedience Brings Consequences

Cursed is the ground for thy sake; in sorrow shalt thou eat of it all the days of thy life.

Genesis 3:17

For dust thou art, and unto dust shalt thou return.

Genesis 3:19

Adam, the son of God, who knew His voice, disobeyed His commandment and ate of the tree of the knowledge of good and evil. The result was that judgement was passed down to Adam and every male figure after him.

Before the fall, Adam had a perfect relationship with God and a light occupation. God had put him into the garden of Eden to dress it and to keep it. Now, however, because of disobedience, the ground was cursed and man's lot was changed to burdensome labor in the very dust he was created from.

Mankind had been in Paradise, living for all eternity because there was no sin. It was a time of innocence. Because Adam disobeyed, mankind now faced physical and spiritual death.

> *Therefore as by the offence of one judgment came upon all men to condemnation; even so by the righteousness of one the free gift came upon all men unto justification of life. For as by one man's disobedience many were made sinners, so by the obedience of one shall many be made righteous.* Romans 5:18-19

Not only was Adam now facing death; the ground he was given to work had been cursed: *"Cursed is the ground for thy sake; in sorrow shalt thou eat of it all the days of thy life"* (Genesis 3:17). Man must now work to bring forth food for his family. He must also provide clothes and shelter for them. Men feel incomplete and inadequate when they are unable to fulfill their role as husband, father, and provider.

Men are to be encouraged and respected in their God-given role, being held accountable to God and his family. The husband needs continuous support and encouragement, first from God, and His Word, but also from his wife, his help meet. The husband's strength hinges upon his relationship with God and his wife. His burden will never be more than he can bear, as God has promised:

> *There hath no temptation taken you but such as is common to man: but God is faithful, who will not suffer you to be tempted above that ye are able.* 1 Corinthians 10:13

The Judgment Passed on Eve

Now let's focus on the judgment passed on Eve for her disobedience. We will examine each important word or phrase of the following verse:

> *Unto the woman he said, I will greatly multiply thy sorrow and thy conception; in sorrow thou shalt bring forth children; and thy desire shall be to thy husband, and he shall rule over you.*
> Genesis 3:16

I will greatly multiply—Hebrew (*raw-baw*) "to

increase in whatever respect; bring in abundance, enlarge, excel, heap, continue, belong."

Thy sorrows — Hebrew (*its-tsaw-bone'*) from (*aw-tsab*) "in a bad sense. To worry, pain or anger, displease, grief, hurt, make, be sorry, vex, wrest."

In sorrow — Hebrew (*eh'-tseb*) "an earthen vessel: usually painful, toil; also pang (whether body or mind) grievous, labor, travail."

Thy desire — Hebrew (*tesh-oo-aw'*) from (*shook*) "to run after or over, overflow, water. Sense of stretching out after; a longing."

Rule — Hebrew (*maw-shal'*) "have, make to have dominion, governor, reign (bear, cause to, have) power, have dominion over, ruler, ruling."

The price to pay when we choose to disobey God affects everyone and everything connected to us. The psalmist David made this very plain when he said:

> *Behold, I was shaped in iniquity; and in sin did my mother conceive me.* Psalm 51:6

Disobedience Brings Consequences

Every woman born to man after Eve has suffered these judgments in some form or fashion.

Even in laughter the heart is sorrowful; and the end of that mirth is heaviness.

Proverbs 14:13

Thy sorrows—examine these scriptures:

- Ecclesiastes 10:9—Physical pain
- 1 Samuel 20:34—Emotional pain
- 1 Chronicles 4:10—Both emotional and physical pain

In sorrow—examine these scriptures:

- Genesis 35:16—*And they journeyed from Bethel; and there was but a little way to come to Ephrath: and Rachel travailed, and she had hard labour.*
- Isaiah 13:8—*Pangs and sorrows shall take hold of them.*
- Isaiah 42:14—*Now I will cry like a woman in travail.*
- John 16:21—*A woman in travail has sorrow and anguish.*

One Flesh

We know that we will be faced with some level of grief, sorrow, pain, and discomfort. Thanks be to God for His Son Jesus who became a curse that we could be free from this curse. We can claim our freedom through faith in His finished work on the cross:

For ye know the grace of our Lord Jesus Christ, that, though he was rich, yet for your sakes he became poor, that ye through his poverty might be rich. 2 Corinthians 8:9

For as many as are of the works of the law are under the curse: for it is written, cursed is every one that continued not in all things which are written in the book of the law to do them. But that no man is justified by the law in the sight of God, it is evident: for, the just shall live by faith. And the law is not of faith: but, the man that doeth them shall live in them. Galatians 3:10-14

For what the law could not do, in that it was weak through the flesh, God sending his own Son in the likeness of sinful flesh, and for sin, condemned sin in the flesh: that the righteousness of the law might be fulfilled in us, who walk

Disobedience Brings Consequences

not after the flesh, but after the spirit.
For to be carnally minded is death; but to be
spiritually minded is life and peace.

Romans 8:3-4 and 6

Yes, through faith in Jesus Christ, those who walk after the Spirit are redeemed from the curse pronounced on Eve in the Garden of Eden. Please note: We are redeemed from the curse of sin and death through the blood of Jesus. This doesn't mean that the law has changed. We must actively submit ourselves wholly to the ordinances God has set:

And thy desire shall be to thy husband, and he
shall rule over thee.   Genesis 3:16

Is Christian marriage exempt from the problems brought on by Adam's disobedience? No! But in Christ Jesus we have all the help we need to become victorious.

Study Questions

1. Do you believe Adam received just judgment for listening to Eve?

2. Do you believe the husband should be responsible for providing for is family? If so, why? If not, why?

3. Can you support your spouse in his or her God-given role and responsibilities?

4. Do you believe that the judgment brought on Eve was too harsh? Why?

5. What could Eve have done to escape the temptation of the serpent?

6. Have you ever found yourself listening to the voice of the serpent?

7. What could you have done to avoid his schemes?

8. What are the mechanisms we can use to confirm the voice of God?

9. Will the serpent ever tell you the truth?

10. What is the sole mission of the serpent? Find the following scripture in your Bible and read what they say: John 8:44, John 10:10 and Revelation 12:9.

Houses and riches are the inheritance of fathers:
and a prudent wife is from the LORD.

Proverbs 19:14

CHAPTER 4

God's Delegated Authority

*But I would have you know, that the head of
every man is Christ; and the head of the woman
is the man; and the head of Christ is God.*

1 Corinthians 11:3

Knowing and understanding your role in marriage
makes it work so much better. First in the line of delegated authority is Christ. Next comes the husband,
then the wife, then the children:

*For the husband is the head of the wife, even as
Christ is the head of the church: and he is the
savior of the body.* Ephesians 5:23

This is the undisputed delegated authority of God
regarding families.

One Flesh

The Role of the Husband

And the LORD God planted a garden eastward in Eden; and there he put the man whom he had formed.
And the LORD God took the man and put him into the garden of Eden to dress [till] it and to keep it.   Genesis 2:8 and 15

Adam knew God as Lord and Master, God gave Adam duties he was to be responsible to carry out, and God would hold Adam accountable for the assigned work. Here, again, we see that before the Lord God gave man a wife, he gave him a job (responsibilities) in the Garden. Man was responsible for the tillage, and because of it, the man was held accountable.

God is a god of precepts, order and principles. His goal was to prepare Adam to function in the capacity he would later be given. We know that God prepares us for what's ahead, the future of His plans and purposes for our lives. God knew Adam would be responsible for caring for His God-given family. His duties would include those of provider, protector and lover, and he would be required to have a commitment, a dependence, a consistency and a loyalty.

God's Delegated Authority

This was all before a wife was even considered. Then the Lord created a wife for Adam, a help meet for him. The Lord took the woman out of man and made her his help meet. In this way, the two of them were equally yoked. They were the same, and yet not the same. They had a certain individuality, and yet they were complimentary. When we allow God to be the Matchmaker, life together is far better than it could be if we tried to put it all together ourselves. He always knows best.

Adam was happy. He declared:

> *And Adam said, this is now bone of my bones, and flesh of my flesh: she shall be called Woman, because she was taken out of Man.*
>
> Genesis 2:23

Adam had respect for Eve. She was a part of his own identity. A woman, a wife, is symbolic of the Church, the Bride of Christ, and we know how much Jesus loves His Church.

Then we come to Genesis 3 and the Fall, and all seems to have been lost. But then we have the promise of redemption (see Genesis 3:1-4:7).

The serpent deceived Eve, Eve persuaded Adam to eat of the forbidden fruit, and humankind suffered

One Flesh

spiritual death and eventually physical death as well. Three individuals were involved in this disaster and all three were issued judgments. These were the consequences of their choices and behaviors. The three characters, of course, were the serpent, Eve and Adam, and all three suffered:

> *And the LORD God said unto the serpent, Because thou hast done this, thou art cursed above all cattle, and above every beast of the field; upon thy belly shalt thou go, and dust shalt thou eat all the days of thy life: and I will put enmity between thee and the woman, and between thy seed and her seed; it shall bruise thy head, and thou shalt bruise his heel.*
>
> *Unto the woman he said, I will greatly multiply thy sorrow and thy conception; in sorrow thou shalt bring forth children; and thy desire shall be to thy husband, and he shall rule over thee.*
>
> *And unto Adam he said, because thou has hearkened unto the voice of thy wife, and hast eaten of the tree, of which I commanded thee, saying, Thou shall not eat of it: cursed is the ground for thy sake; in sorrow shalt thou eat of it all the days of thy life; thorns also and thistles shall it bring forth to thee; and thou shall eat the herb*

of the field; in the sweat of thy face shalt thou eat bread, till thou return unto the ground; for out of it wast thou taken; for dust thou art, and unto dust shalt thou return. Genesis 3:14-19

The Lord God here reiterated to Adam (and to every man after him) the description of his position. It was, first, leader, ruler, protector and, then, provider. The word *rule* in the Hebrew is (*maw-shal'*) meaning "to have, make to have dominion, governor, reign (bear, cause to, have) power, have dominion over, ruler, ruling."

We see that a man must work the ground that is now cursed because of disobedience. Adam was now out working to provide for food, shelter and clothing, while Eve was at home attending to the household and the children. But, please note: a woman's duties are never to be looked upon as defamatory in any sense of the word. Hers is a position delegated by God Himself for His own purposes and reasoning.

Under the Edenic Covenant, Adam had six obligations (see Genesis 1:27-31):

- To replenish the earth with children
- To use nature for his physical needs, including food and shelter

- To have dominion over the animal life
- To eat fruit and vegetables
- To labor for his sustenance
- To obey the commandments of God[4]

Again, God gave Adam a job before He brought forth his wife (see Genesis 2:15). It is vital that a man have substance or means to provide for a wife and children. Working hard and making an honest living is how a man is wired. It is his makeup. Anything less would make him feel inadequate, inferior and insecure. Man is the ultimate provider of the home. He is the protector. He protects his wife, his children, his home, and his finances.

The husband, with the assistance of the wife, is responsible for the family's safety and health. For instance: health insurance, prescription drugs, dental insurance, ophthalmologist, education, extra-curricular activities ... and the list goes on. This includes clothing, footwear, eyewear, etc.

The husband is in authority. In any group, there is a boss, a master, a leader, a supervisor or chief. Every other person in that same group is known as a subordinate. *Subordinate* means "placed in or occupying a lower class, rank, or position, submissive to or controlled by authority." Subordinates

4. The Scofield Study Bible (Oxford, UK, Oxford University Press: 2003)

are those who come after or beneath. Notice that it does not mean *less than*, but is an order of ranking. *Husband*, in the Hebrew, (*essh*), means "a man as an individual or a male person." *Husband* in the Greek (*an-ayr*), means "a man (as an individual male) fellow, husband, sir."

For other aspects of the husband's position, we will look at passages from the New Testament. There the writings of the apostles Paul and Peter adequately describe the duties of both husband and wife, confirming God's original delegated authority:

For the husband is the head of the wife, even as Christ is the head of the church: and he is the saviour of the body. Therefore as the church is subject unto Christ, so let the wives be to their own husbands in every thing.

Husbands, love your wives, even as Christ also loved the church, and gave himself for it; that he might sanctify and cleanse it with the washing of water by the word, that he might present it to himself a glorious church, not having spot, or wrinkle, or any such thing; but that it should be holy and without blemish. So ought men to love their wives as their own bodies. He that loveth his wife loveth himself. For no man ever yet hated

One Flesh

*his own flesh; but nourisheth and cherisheth it,
even as the Lord the church: for we are members
of his body, of his flesh, and of his bones. For this
cause shall a man leave his father and mother, and
shall be joined unto his wife, and they two shall
be one flesh. This is a great mystery: but I speak
concerning Christ and the church. Nevertheless
let every one of you in particular so love his wife
even as himself; and the wife see that she reverence
her husband.*   Ephesians 5:23-33

So the husband is to love his wife as Christ loved
the Church. Christ loved the Church in the past, He
loves the Church today, and He will always love the
Church. His love for the Church is past, present and
future. It is never ending. That is how a man should
love his wife. He should love her as he loves his own
body. He who loves his wife loves himself:

*For no man ever yet hated his own flesh; but
nourisheth and cherisheth it, even as the Lord
the church.*   Ephesians 5:29

Just as a man respects, nurtures and cares for his
own body, so must he do for his wife. She is part of
his being. The two of them are one flesh.

God's Delegated Authority

Most marital conflicts stem from failure of the husband or wife or both to submit to Christ, spend time in His Word and seek to do His will each day. This explains why a Christian should marry a Christian and not become *"unequally yoked together"* with an unbeliever (2 Corinthians 6:14). If the Christian is submitted to Christ, he will not try to establish a home that disobeys the Word of God.

A Christian couple must be careful to submit to Christ's Lordship even before they are married. Unless the couple prays together and sincerely seeks God's will in His Word, their marriage begins on a weak foundation.[5]

---

5. Wiersbe, Warren W., *Be Rich* (Colorado Springs, CO, David C. Cook: 1979)

Study Questions

1. What does it mean to you that the husband should be head of the wife and family?

2. What are the purposes of a husband?

3. What evidence do you see that lets you know your partner is ready to fulfill his role of a husband?

4. If none, list those qualifications that are missing.

5. How might knowing the truth about what God expects from us change your decisions?

For this cause shall a man leave his father and mother, and shall be joined unto his wife, and they two shall be one flesh. This is a mystery: but I speak concerning Christ and the church.

God's Delegated Authority

The Role of the Wife

God said to Eve:

And he shall rule over thee. Genesis 3:16

Why? God wants to protect us women from the schemes of the enemy. Adam was not deceived:

And Adam was not deceived, but the woman being deceived was in the transgression.
1 Timothy 2:14

Through judgment, Eve and all women after her became subordinate to their own husbands. Eve and all women after her were to suffer in childbearing and child-rearing.

Wife in Hebrew (*ish-shaw'*) means "female." In the Greek (*gune' or goo-nay*) "a woman or wife." As we have seen, God said:

Whoso findeth a wife findeth a good thing, and obtaineth favor of the LORD. Proverbs 18:22

Peter wrote to the early church believers:

One Flesh

Likewise, ye husbands, dwell with them with understanding, giving honor unto the wife, as unto the weaker vessel. 1 Peter 3:7

Remember, his wife is his "help meet," a helper comparable to him and working alongside of him. "A help (meet) aid, help, from surround, protect, or helper, relief (see Genesis 2:18)."

The wife must be in subjection to her own husband, and she is one who will bring forth children and keep her house (see Titus 2:1-6). The wife is also a builder of her home (see Proverbs 14:1). She is working with her husband, and their acts are synchronized and choreographed according to the will of the Father. She may not be on the job *with* him, but she is at her assigned location, working hard for the success of their marriage, home and family.

Solomon declared:

A wise [prudent] *wife is from the* LORD.
Proverbs 19:14

A wise wife seeks counsel from more mature Christian women. I would also suggest that she prays for God to provide her with a spiritual mother. What is a spiritual mother? A spiritual mother is someone who fears God, prays without ceasing for everyone and everything, has a good reputation in the community, loves unconditionally and operates in black and white. Because she loves people, she also correct them, directs them and supports them. She is a teacher of good and holy things, and she teaches younger women how to care for their husbands and how to keep their children and their home.

I have had a couple of spiritual mothers. Although they are no longer with me, their wisdom still speaks. I thank God for allowing them to cross my path.

In Titus 2, Paul tells us how we ought to behave in the home. Submission starts with respect. We submit, first, to God and His order because we reverence Him. In the same way, a wife must have reverence for the man in authority over her.

In Romans 13, Paul spoke of submission. Unfortunately, our modern world has a bad concept of this word and its meaning. Today *submitting* or *submission* is a very controversial subject. It is most often frowned upon. The reason is that our modern generations fail to understand the spiritual purpose of submission. You and I are not children of the world, that we should obey the lusts thereof. We are children of an everlasting Kingdom.

One Flesh

During Jesus' ministry on the earth, everywhere He went, there were controversies because Truth always threatens tradition, wrong mindsets, and accepted religious precepts. The Scriptures let us know that there are certain authorities we should always submit to: God, our parents, those in authority over us, and wives to their own husbands.

Submission actually refers to a place or position. It comes from a Greek word *hupotasso,* which literally means "to place under, to arrange in an orderly fashion, or to assign position." I like to say, "Submission is a place of protection, purpose and provision." God is protecting His Bride, at the same time providing for her so that she can bring forth His divine purpose.

In Ephesian 5:22-24, Paul gives two reasons for this command: the Lordship of Christ (v. 22) and the headship of the man in Christ (v. 23). When the Christian wife submits herself to Christ and lets Him be the Lord of her life, she will have no difficulty submitting to her husband.

This does not mean that she becomes a slave, for the husband is also to submit to Christ. And if both are living under the Lordship of Christ, there can be only harmony. Headship is not dictatorship. "Each for the other, both for the Lord."[6]

6. Wiersbe, Warren W., *Be Rich* (Colorado Springs, CO, David C. Cook: 1979)

God's Delegated Authority

A wife should be pure, the wife of one husband. She should be adorned with the spirit of meekness and a quiet spirit, which is of great price in the sight of God (see 1 Peter 3:4). Peter was suggesting that the wife wear "meekness" as an accessory, to make herself more attractive. God is interested in the hidden man of the heart, not so much the outward appearance. Therefore, meekness, as an accessory, should never be left off. The spirit of meekness beautifies whoever chooses to wear it.

A wife should not be loud and contentious:

> *But a foolish woman is clamorous; she is simple, and knoweth nothing.*   Proverbs 9:13

> *She is loud and stubborn; her feet abide not in her house.*   Proverbs 7:11

> *It is better to dwell in the wilderness, than with a contentious and an angry woman.* Proverbs 21:19

Study these scriptures thoroughly to gain knowledge and understanding, and may the grace of God grant you wisdom to apply their message to your life. Here are a few more:

One Flesh

It is better to dwell in a corner of the housetop, than with a brawling woman in a wide house.
Proverbs 21:9

Every wise woman buildeth her house: but the foolish plucketh it down with her hands. Proverbs 14:1

Through wisdom is an house builded; and by understanding it is established. Proverbs 24:36

We read in Esther 1:1-17 how the queen before Esther forfeited her crown through an act of defiance. Her name was Queen Vashti, and she had duties and responsibilities, not only to her husband in the God-ordained order in the role of a wife; she also had the duties of a queen, a very high and influential position.

During a certain time of the year when the king would meet with all of his princes, the queen and all the princesses of the land, there were celebrations which went on for weeks.

On the seventh day, when the heart of the king was merry with wine, he commanded Mehuman, Biztha, Harbona, Bigtha, and Abagtha, Zethar, and Carcas, the seven chamberlains that served in the presence of Ahasuerus the king, to bring Vashti the queen before the king with the crown royal, to shew the people and the princes her beauty: for she was fair to look on.

Esther 1:10-11

But, strangely, the queen refused to come forth as the king had commanded:

But the queen Vashti refused to come at the king's commandment by his chamberlains: therefore was the king very wroth, and his anger burned in him. Esther 1:12

Vashti's first role was that of wife, and then she was subject, like anyone else, to the king's commandments. For some reason, she chose to violate those commands. So she was either a disobedient wife or a defiant queen, and neither was acceptable. Her behavior was dealt with in no uncertain terms, so that there would be no more disobedience in the land.

The king sought counsel of his wisest men, *"which knew the times"* (Esther 1:13):

And Memucan answered before the king and the princes, Vashti the queen hath not done wrong to the king only, but also to all the princes, and

One Flesh

*to all the people that are in all the provinces of
the king Ahasuerus. For this deed of the queen
shall come abroad unto all women, so that they
shall despise their husbands in their eyes, when
it shall be reported, The king Ahasuerus commanded Vashti the queen to be brought in before
him, but she came not.*   Esther 1:16-17

Disobedience has had its consequences from
the Garden of Eden until now. Queen Vashti
had a choice, and she chose to defy her duties
as a wife and also as Queen of the nation. As a
result, she lost her crown to another, who was
both beautiful and humble. Queen Esther soon
succeeded her. It is important for both of you to
understand your roles and duties, and, equally important, to submit to those in authority.

The Bible doesn't say why Queen Vashti refused
to comply. It is not relevant. What the Bible shows
is that her negligence cost her the crown. Soon a
decree went forth:

*If it please the king, let there go a royal com-
mandment from him, and let it be written
among the laws of the Persians and the Medes,
that it be not altered, that Vashti come no more*

68

before king Ahasuerus; and let the king give her royal estate unto another that is better than she.   Esther 1:19

Paul wrote to the churches:

Wives, submit yourselves unto your own husbands, as unto the Lord. For the husband is the head of the wife, even as Christ is the head of the church: and he is the saviour of the body. Therefore as the church is subject unto Christ, so let the wives be to their own husbands in every thing.   Ephesians 5:22-24

The wife is the maker of the home with the support of her husband. Her home is to be a safe place, a place of comfort, nurturing, protection, understanding, assurance and wise counsel.

Study Questions

1. Have you given thought to the type of spouse you desire to become?

2. Are you actively behaving as the spouse a man will desire to have as his wife, his life-long partner?

3. Are you a wise and prudent woman?

4. Are you willing to learn to be the wife God and your husband will be pleased to look upon?

5. Are you desiring to be the wife who makes your husband and children rise up and call you blessed?

6. How do you feel about Queen Vashti losing her crown to another?

7. Can you justify Queen Vashti's behavior?

8. If you are justifying an act of disobedience, why?

CHAPTER 5

Being Equally Yoked

> *Be ye not unequally yoked together with unbelievers: for what fellowship hath righteousness with unrighteousness? and what communion hath light with darkness?* 2 Corinthians 6:14

What does it mean to be *"unequally yoked together"*? The definition from Strong's 2086 is "Greek (*heterozygéō*) "mis-matched" and is used figuratively of Christians wrongly committed to a partner holding very different values or priorities. One desires to further God's Kingdom, but the other holds values that run contrary to faith in God.

Being yoked to someone or something that does not line up with the principles of God becomes a burden, not a blessing. It is strenuous and counterproductive. The opposing spouse seems to be going their own way, pulling and stretching you to a place you have no desire to be. Under a yoke, the strongest will do all the directing and the leading. As Christian husband and wife, we must walk together and pull together toward victory in our marriage, our relationship and our home.

Ruth made a covenant with Naomi:

> *And they lifted up their voice, and wept again: and Orpah kissed her mother in law; but Ruth clave unto her. And she said, Behold, thy sister in law is gone back unto her people, and unto her gods: return thou after thy sister in law. And Ruth said, Intreat me not to leave thee, or to return from following after thee: for whither thou goest, I will go; and where thou lodgest, I will lodge: thy people shall be my people, and thy God my God: where thou diest, will I die, and there will I be buried: the Lord do so to me, and more also, if ought but death part thee and me.* Ruth 1:14-17

It's all about a covenant between two parties. Is your God my god? Will you serve my God? Will you live among my people? Will you support me in every circumstance?

Being Equally Yoked

Husbands and wives will share in many things as they venture through life together. Unless they do it as one flesh, they will be working at cross purposes. Jesus taught:

> *For this cause shall a man leave father and mother and shall cleave to his wife: and they twain* [the two] *shall be one flesh. Wherefore they are no more twain, but one flesh. What therefore God hath joined together, let not man put asunder.* Matthew 19:5-6

We see that, based upon the Scriptures, the man and the woman should agree. The importance of this cannot be overstated. It is hard, if not impossible, for two people to walk together, except they be agreed, as the prophet Amos declared:

> *Can two walk together, except they be agreed?* Amos 3:3

God warned the children of Israel to separate themselves from non-believers, which in Old Testament days, were called "heathen." These heathen and their practices of worshiping idols eventually ensnared many of the children of Israel. God also warned the children of Israel against giving their sons or daughters in marriage to unbelievers:

Thou shalt make no covenant with them, nor show mercy unto them: neither shalt thou make marriages with them; thy daughter thou shalt not give unto his son, nor his daughter shalt thou take unto they son. For they will turn away thy son from following me that they may serve other gods: so will the anger of the LORD be kindled against you and destroy thee suddenly.

Deuteronomy 7:2-4

King Solomon was a man of uncommon wisdom and great favor with God, but he had one serious flaw: he loved women, particularly those with whom he should have had no dealing, according to the ordinances of God. Solomon not only married heathen women; he began to build temples for their pagan gods. Eventually, these women, who knew nothing of the God of Israel, begin to turn the heart of Solomon to serve their graven images, their gods. Solomon had been warned, but he failed to heed the counsel of God.

Eventually, because Solomon was unequally yoked with unbelieving women and because of his appetite to please them and his own carnal side, it cost him his kingdom. God stripped him of his rule (see 1 Kings 11:1-5 and 14).

Jesus demanded obedience from His disciples:

Jesus said to his disciples, If ye love me, keep my commandments.   John 14:15

To obey is better than to sacrifice (see 1 Samuel 15:22). Obey the Word, rather than sacrificing your salvation and destroying your relationship with the Father. Without the Father's presence, there is no peace and no joy. What good is laughter that leaves an emptiness on the inside of you?

When my friend Linda married Joe, now her ex-husband, he had not received Christ as Lord over his life. She was saved, but even after they were married, he refused to submit his life to Christ.

Linda knew the Word of God well, and she knew that God said, *"Be ye not unequally yoked together with unbelievers."* But, like many, she thought that if Joe really loved her, and she showed him love and respect, he would surely come to Christ afterward. God would surely change his heart; he would be saved, and they could live happily ever after. But those things that Linda prayed for and longed for never happened during the eighteen years of her marriage, and it eventually ended in divorce.

God means just what He says. He is all-wise and all-knowing. He knows the end of all men, and He will not compromise His Word for you, nor will He compromise it for me.

God is just and righteous always, and His Word will not conform to our standards. We must conform to His Word. In order to walk successfully together, we must be equally yoked.

When you think about marriages like Linda's, there was never any real union. *Union* means "an act or instance of uniting or joining two or more things into one; especially the formation of a single political unit from two or more separate and individual units." What Linda and Joe tried to make work could never have worked.

Linda disobeyed the Word of God, and therefore, she had to suffer the consequences. She testified of many sleepless nights, many doctor's visits and even a bout with cancer. Because of the abuse she suffered, her health took a downward spiral. Yes, she suffered emotional abuse, psychological abuse, verbal abuse, betrayal, and many incidents of infidelity during the course of the marriage.

Being Equally Yoked

The strongman of jealousy gripped Joe and he would accuse Linda of having affairs with every man passing by, whether that man was walking or crawling, in a wheelchair or in a coma. Joe was a sick man, and he took out his sickness on Linda. When you are without Christ, you are without hope.

Linda could not remember when there had been a decent conversation between them, one that ended on a good note. Someone who is spiritually blind cannot see where the Spirit-filled man is going, nor can they communicate. Spiritual things are spiritually discerned.

When Linda got home from church each week, she was verbally abused. She was degraded with false accusations all that evening and sometimes throughout the next week.

Thankfully, Linda knew where to find peace and strength, but her torments finally ended in divorce. Why did it happen? Because God didn't put that couple together. Linda did it ... in disobedience to the Word of God.

Joe is still not saved today. Linda has been liberated from her bondage and is consistently walking in the will and the love of God, bringing Him glory.

In closing this chapter, let us see our theme verse in full context:

One Flesh

Be ye not unequally yoked together with un-believers; for what fellowship (communion) hath righteousness with unrighteousness? And what communion hath light with darkness? And what concord [harmony or agreement] *hath Christ with Belial? Or what part hath he that believe with an infidel* [unbeliever]. *And what agreement hath the temple of God with idols? For ye are the temple of the living God; as God hath said, I will dwell in them, and walk in them, and I will be their God, and they shall be my people. Wherefore come out from among them, and be ye separate, saith the Lord, and touch not the unclean thing; and I will receive you, and will be a Father unto you, and ye shall be my sons and daughters, saith the Lord Almighty,* 2 Corinthians 6:14-18

Study Questions

1. What price are you willing to pay to walk in disobedience?

2. Have you ever been in a relationship where you both were headed in opposite directions?

3. If so, what was the outcome of that relationship?

4. Are you and your partner equally yoked?

5. Are you both worshipping and serving the same God?

6. How can we, as partners, serve different gods?

7. If you are unequally yoked, what is it that keeps pulling you in different directions? And how will you fix it?

CHAPTER 6

Mastering Communication Etiquette

*But let your communication be, Yea, yea; Nay,
nay: for whatsoever is more than these cometh
of evil.* Matthew 5:37

On the list of things that cause divorce, one of the big items is lack of communication. What is communication? As a noun, it is "an act of transmitting; message; exchange of information of opinions, a means of communicating." As a verb, *to communicate*, it means "to make known; to pass from one to another; transmit: to receive communion; to be in communication; join, connect; a dialogue between two or more people; exchange of information."

When we need to talk openly and honestly about something difficult with another person, we must focus on the conversation with keen attention and purpose. During the conversation, we must listen patiently, speak tactfully, and tell the truth as we understand it. We must align our words, voice inflection and tone, eye expression, body language and actions with our inner awareness in an honest exchange.

An effective communicator is described as having these traits: is a good listener, one who does not interrupt, one who makes eye contact, one who understands how body language can affect how information is being transmitted, one who is open minded, one who never starts a statement with "You ... ." Make sure the person you plan to spend the rest of your life with is able and willing to effectively communicate.

Communication skills are a must in decision-making. Do not settle for "it's just the way he or she is." That is a cover-up of what to expect after marriage. Do not buy that. If the person is that way now—unwilling to communicate—he or she will be that way during the marriage. If you are a communicator and your spouse-to-be is not, this is something you must seriously consider before you say, "I do."

Communication is the basis for transmitting information, and without it you have chaos. Many people make the mistake of going into marriage to change someone into becoming the mate they desire. Please don't deceive yourself. A man or woman cannot change another for the better. When we go into marriage not accepting the person for who they really are, we set ourselves up for disappointment, failure and resentment.

Why do I say that? First, we are putting our expectations on others. Second, you married the person for what you believed that person should become (not accepting the reality of what they are now). God alone has the ability to change someone into a better individual and, for that to happen, they have to sincerely want to change.

If you are fond of someone who wears a size ten dress, why would you marry someone who wears a size twelve dress? You married someone with short hair, but you love a person with long hair, so during the marriage you bring up, at every opportunity, how you wish she would let her hair grow longer. You married a person who is people friendly and talks with everyone they meet, and then you get upset and jealous when they do. Why? You have not accepted the person for who they are. Instead, you have set in your mind (your imagination) that they will change to accommodate you. Well, that probably will not happen, and this sets the stage for contention, strife, anger, disrespect and infidelity.

One Flesh

A good communicator will allow others to express their thoughts, while actively listening. A good communicator will allow the other person to finish talking without interrupting them. A good communicator will not escalate a conversation to make a point. A good communicator will always ask for clarity and not make assumptions. A good communicator is always aware of his or her own body language as being part of the conversation. A good communicator will not force an issue, but will allow for a cool-down period if necessary.

It is imperative for the two of you to communicate in a marriage, for this is the normal means of sharing information. Some will talk a lot, and others will say only what is necessary to get the point across to the next person. Some people will not talk unless they have a couple of glasses of wine (or a whole bottle). Please be aware: if the person you are interested in marrying cannot communicate unless they are under the influence of some type of mood-altering chemical, I would suggest that you seriously seek the Lord for His divine direction before you say, "I do."

Boundaries are laid in communication. "No" is the most basic boundary-setting word, yet, it is also a confrontational word. Being clear about your "no" and your "yes" is a theme that runs throughout the Bible. James taught:

> *But above all things, my brethren, swear not, neither by heaven, neither by the earth, neither by any other oath: but let your yea be yea; and your nay, nay; lest ye fall into condemnation.* James 5:12

We must know how to say "no" when we are sinfully treated (see Matthew 18:15-20).

Christians must never be under the control of wine or other mood-altering drugs, but should be filled with the Spirit of God. My good friend Linda testified that while she and her husband were dating, he was a good talker, especially when he had a couple of beers or a half pint of gin. And Linda is a great conversationalist. But after they married, she spent a lot of time alone, not being able to share with Joe. It was hard to share with him, because there was no effective dialogue between them. Joe was not comfortable expressing his feelings, and he often got upset when he felt lost during a conversation. Remember, you must be equally yoked:

One Flesh

For what communion hath a believer with an unbeliever or what communion light has with darkness. 1 Corinthians 6:14

A poor communicator will demonstrate these behaviors: a passive mood (I'm not talking), withdrawal, silence, pouting, escalation, or will go so far as not to attend to personal duties, etc. Non-verbal behaviors are just as destructive as verbal ones. Neither will help the situation, but will only prolong the issue, giving Satan a foothold.

Learn to communicate effectively. Be honest and respectful. Listen well to your mate, and watch your body language:

> *To whom ye forgive anything, I forgive also: for if I forgave anything, to whom I forgave it, for your sakes forgave I it in the person of Christ; lest Satan should get an advantage of us: for we are not ignorant of his devices.* 2 Corinthians 2:10-11

Proverbs 15 and Its Important Lessons in Communication

One very important part of communication is the ability to turn away wrath:

Mastering Communication Etiquette

A soft answer turneth away wrath: but griev-
ous words stir up anger. The tongue of the
wise useth knowledge aright: but the mouth
of fools poureth out foolishness.

Proverbs 15:1-2

Always give way to the Spirit of God. Be quick to listen, but slow to respond. Think about what you want to say before opening your mouth. Here are some other general rules for great communication supported by this important chapter of Proverbs 15:

1. Remain calm and gentle when confronting conflict, and your example will become contagious (see verse 1).
2. Speak wisely, making sure your information is truthful and accurate (see verse 2).
3. Remember, God is the ultimate Judge and will execute justice (see verse 3).
4. Use your words to foster healing; fix the problem, not the blame (see verse 4).
5. Stay teachable; be open to correction and quick to apologize when wrong (see verse 5).
6. Add value to everyone who contacts you, even when you disagree (see verse 6).

7. Speak words that spread knowledge and understanding, showing love, compassion and mercy (see verse 7). [7]

---

7. Adapted from the *NKJV Maxwell Leadership Bible* copyright 2002, 2007, 218 by Maxwell Motivation, Inc.

Study Questions

1. What type of communicator are you?

2. How do you deal with disagreements?

3. Are you passive, hoping the issue will just go away?

4. Do you or your partner communicate only after you have a drink or some other type of mood-altering chemical?

5. Do you believe someone is asking for an argument when they say they want to discuss some issue or other? Why?

6. Why is it important to effectively communicate?

7. What happens when voices begin to be raised during communication? Why?

8. Have you discussed your goals and desires with your prospective mate? If not, why not?

CHAPTER 7

Avoiding Surprises

For there is nothing hid, which shall not be manifested; neither was any thing kept secret, but that it should come abroad.   Mark 4:22

Here are some topics that must be discussed with your potential partner before you get too serious in your relationship:

- Any previous relationships
- Any previous marriages
- How each marriage ended
- Are there alimony payments?
- How much and how often?
- How long has it been since the last breakup in a relationship?

One Flesh

In the case of marriages that ended because of your partner's choice, you might want to pray more about committing to a long life with this person.

You must also discuss children:
- Are there any children?
- Is there a possibility of a child being born soon?
- If there are children, is there child support?
- If child support is required, what are the payment arrangements? How much must be paid and how often?
- Who has custody?
- Who has visitation rights?
- What are the frequency of those visitations?
- What other guidelines have been ordered?

Make sure your potential partner has had ample time to heal from past relationships. Ask:
- What was the last time they visited or talked?
- When was their last date?

Ask financial questions:
- His or her current credit status?
- Credit scores?
- Any bankruptcies?
- Any charge-offs?

Avoiding Surprises

- Any IRS debt?
- Any remaining student loans?
- Any credit cards and/or other active loans?

Ask medical questions:
- His or her medical history
- Is his or her health excellent, good or poor?
- Does he or she have health insurance?
- Are there pre-existing health problems and, if so, how long have they existed?
- What is the history of hereditary diseases (like sickle cell anemia, cancer and heart disease)?
- What is the history of mental health in his or her family and in him or her specifically?
- Is there a history of depression?
- Have there ever been any suicide attempts?
- Has there been any drug or alcohol abuse?

This list is far from conclusive. Let the Spirit of God lead you in your questions.

Also ask about this person's criminal history:

- How many arrests?
- What were the charges (DWI, Drug Possession, Battery, Theft, etc.)

- What is the current status of each case (Probation or Parole, etc.)?
- Have there ever been any child-abuse, sexual-abuse or marital-abuse charges?

This need-to-know list might seem invasive and intrusive, and it is meant to be that way. If you are planning to spend the rest of your life with a person, you should at least know these things. This is the very minimum.

Don't be caught by surprise by any of these because you feel "It's their business, and it should be kept that way." If you say this, you are being naïve, and if you're not careful, something listed here will surprise you.

You might be saying, "This is not the right timing." What better time could there be? Do this now, before you say, "I do." Why? There are many reasons.

Here is one example. If you marry and have a child and that child is born with sickle cell anemia or some other genetic issue, the hospital waiting room is not the place to learn that your partner has sickle cell anemia. Ask plenty of questions before you say " I do" and save yourself and everyone else a lot of headaches or battles with health issues.

Children from previous marriages tend to be a

stressor on a marriage. Find out all you can before you commit. Committing to a spouse is committing to his whole family. And you will have to deal with his or her ex-partners as well.

Finances is one of the top three reasons why people divorce. You want to know about your partners financial background, whether he or she is an investor or a spender. Is it your desire to live from paycheck to paycheck because you married someone who thinks it's okay to party every payday and not be responsible? Or do you desire a spouse who plans because he or she understands the reason for budgeting? This is a serious issue. Consider it well.

Study Questions

1. How important is it for you to know about your partner's past and present, especially regarding previous relationships?

2. If your partner has children from a previous relationship, have you discussed the arrangements?

3. How important is it for you to know your partner's mental, medical and financial status?

4. Are you willing to discuss family history and even genetic issues?

5. Are you willing to raise a family with your partner, knowing his or her family history?

CHAPTER 8

Considering Cultural Diversity

By these were the isles of the Gentiles divided in their lands; every one after his tongue, after their families, in their nations. Genesis 10:5

We all come with different backgrounds and cultures, and when varied cultures mix in marriage, this requires respect and understanding to be able to avoid endless wars and chaos. I've had the privilege of living among different ethnicities and learning of differing cultures, and I can say that what an American-born person would say about their grandparents, for example, is totally different from what a Chinese, Indian or Mexican would say. Therefore, in a cross-cultural marriage, it is very important to learn about your partner's culture. This shows respect to them and to their relatives and friends.

How does culture affect our communication style? Have you thought about it? Communication and culture have a great influence on any individual. Past experiences, perception and cultural background greatly affect the way people talk and behave. Culture plays an important role in shaping the style of communication.

Some examples of cultural barriers are religious practices (as mentioned before). The differences in values and beliefs forms a cultural barrier. Body language and gestures are other elements of the cultural barrier.

Cultural differences will affect and influence how individuals in intimate relationships communicate. These norms also affect other behaviors and attitudes that significantly affect relationships.

It is the responsibility of both the man and the woman to investigate the other's culture before entering a marriage covenant. If, after you have learned, you feel you can still embrace the differences, then educate yourself and have patience, as you discuss with your partner how to make the marriage work. Learn to be tolerant, learn the language that will help you to communicate in a better way. All of this will help you prepare to make a commitment to marriage.

Considering Cultural Diversity

Cultural differences not only affect a relationship, but most everything else about it. For example, what do you eat when each partner has grown up with a different diet. Some foods are not tolerated by certain ethnic groups. For example, those with an Irish heritage have a higher possibility of contracting celiac disease, a disorder of the small intestines that causes damage when wheat, barley or rye products are eaten. If you didn't know this and yet continued to prepare meals containing these products, it could cause big problems — medically and financially.

Another example would be to assume that all Jews don't eat pork. Jewishness is an ethnicity as well as a religion. Religious Jews don't eat pork, but many ethnic Jews do. What a big headache it would be to try to appease a spouse you knew and understood little about! You can't afford to let that happen.

Rearing children is another big difference among the various cultures. Some Americans allow their children to rebel and talk back, but among other nationalities this is a cause for severe punishment. What do you think of this?

Even among people of the same ethnicity and cultural traditions, marriage presents many occasions for differing opinions and hurt feelings. How much more when a man and woman of diverse background are joined in marriage. Do yourself the favor of learning all you can learn about the person you hope to marry and, when it comes to cultural differences, make sure you will be able to live in peace with one another before you make a formal commitment to the marriage.

Study Questions

1. How are you and your partner different? In background? Ethnicity? Belief?

2. Which holidays and festivals will you be able to attend together without causing grief?

3. What do you know about his or her practices and belief system?

4. How important are family gatherings to you both?

5. How important is helping an elderly parent to you both?

6. What agreement have you and your partner reached concerning child discipline? (The Scriptures command us to discipline our children: *"The rod and reproof give wisdom: but a child left to himself bringeth his mother to shame,"* Proverbs 29:15).

7. What are the differences in your beliefs?

8. Have you come to an agreement about how your children should be reared? If not, why not?

9. Do the two of you agree that parents should stand together with rules and resulting discipline concerning their child?

10. Do you agree that a child should be permitted to talk back to a parent or another adult?

11. Do you agree that your child should be held accountable to authority figures?

12. Do you agree that a child should be taught to obey those in authority?

13. Do you believe that any reservation you or your partner have concerning rearing your children will just work itself out without your involvement?

14. Do you agree that leaving the child to his own devices would be an act of negligence?

15. How can your body language be a barrier in your marriage?

16. Are you willing to change your attitudes and behaviors to make your marriage work.

CHAPTER 9

Practicing Honesty and Trust

*That we may lead a quiet and peaceable life in
all godliness and honesty.*   1 Timothy 2:2

Trust ... what is it? As a noun, the word *trust* means
"1. Assured reliance on the character, strength or truth
of someone or something; 2. A basis of reliance, faith
or hope; 3. Confident hope; 4. Financial credit; 5. A
property interest held by one person for the benefit of
another; 6. A combination of firms formed by a legal
agreement, especially one that reduces competition;
7. Something entrusted to one to be cared for in the
interest of another; 8. Care or custody."

As a verb, the word *trust* means "1. To place confidence, depend; 2. To be confident, hope; 3. Entrust;
4. To permit to stay or go or to do something without
fear or misgiving; 5. To rely on or on the truth of,
believe; 6. To extend credit to."

One Flesh

Honesty ... what is it? The word honesty means "Free from deception; truthful; genuine, real, reputable, creditable, marked by integrity, frank."

Christians should embody the characteristics of Christ, and He is truly trustworthy and honest. Both of these characteristics are measured by the amount of information a person is entrusted with and the integrity of how that information is kept.

Before someone can trust you, they must get to know you. We trust God more as we get to know more about Him through Christ and the revealing power of the Holy Spirit, and the same is true with other individuals. This is especially important when it comes to a person you plan to marry. You need to know them well enough to develop a trust between you.

We get to know more about God the Father as we spend time in His Word and in prayer. Spending this time together is a privilege of fellowship and communion for all believers, and we all need more of it. The same can be said about your intended mate. How often do you fellowship with his or her family and friends? This is a strategic way to learn more about that individual and the people close to them. Observing your spouse-to-be while he or she interacts with others in different situations—seeing how they respond, how they problem-solve, and the way they process situations—is important. Some families show love by touching each other, and some don't. Some show love by hugging, kissing and embracing each other, while others don't. In this way, you can tell a lot about what you might expect if you decide to marry this person.

Family history is very important to those who are planning to build a family together. Families love talking about their family accomplishments, and some will discuss failures and disappointments. Visiting your partner's families and friends can open to you a totally different outlook than you may have anticipated. As mentioned already, if you are planning on rearing children together, you want to know some things about the family medical health history, mental health history and social history. Don't be lax and think that this will all take care of itself; it won't. Learn all that you can before you make a serious commitment.

As noted, it is important to know about any troubles with the justice system, any charges pending, any past charges and their outcome, whether they were felonies or misdemeanors. This will all affect your ability to get into certain housing areas, landing that once-in-a-lifetime job or receiving federal benefits if one of you decides to return to college. It

One Flesh

is important to know if there is any criminal background.

You can verify where your partner has traveled by doing an international background check. If your partner seems unwilling to divulge any of this information, you might want to think twice about making a serious life commitment to them.

Once you know more about an individual and ascertain that he or she has a willingness to serve God without reservation, is honest, trustworthy and loyal, then you can feel more at peace about fully committing your life to them. As Christ and the Church, so is the husband and the wife.

Study Questions

1. What is your understanding of trust?

2. Can you trust someone you don't know?

3. How much do you know about your partner?

4. Is there anything in your past you have intentionally kept your partner from discovering?

5. Why are you hiding your past?

6. Do you believe your partner will stop loving you if the truth comes out?

7. Can you honestly repeat your wedding vows, knowing that there are things hidden?

8. Do you think it's best to lie to avoid confrontation?

CHAPTER 10

Living in Harmony

*Submitting yourselves one to another in the fear
of God.*   Ephesians 5:21

Spirit-filled believers are commanded to walk and
live in harmony with each other. Harmony requires
some very important characteristics, which the
apostle Paul has spelled out for us in Ephesians 5.

Be Filled with the Spirit

*And be not drunk with wine, wherein is excess;
but be filled with the Spirit.* Ephesians 5:18

Christians should be filled with the Spirit. Are
you and your partner both filled with the Spirit of
God? Strong drink or wine is a temporary fix for
making a lifelong commitment, but if you are led by

the Spirit of God, you will not fulfill the lusts of the flesh. The Spirit of Truth will lead and guide you; He will comfort you; He will counsel you; He will encourage you; He will teach you the way; He will give you victory over sin (see Galatians 5:17-26).

Be Grateful

Giving thanks always for all things unto God and the Father in the name of our Lord Jesus Christ. Ephesians 5:20

Christians are to be grateful people. Are you and your partner really grateful in all things, praising God and giving Him thanks for whatever comes your way? A true Christian is grateful, not complaining, but rather giving thanks. We trust God with every fiber of our being, and we know that He cares for us. We are, therefore, not anxious people:

Be careful for nothing; but in everything by prayer and supplication with thanksgiving let your requests be known unto God. Philippians 4:6

Have the two of you been praying together, making your requests known to God? Have you been asking for direction and the divine will of God for your lives? When we pray, committing our ways to God, we can then be at peace:

> *And the peace of God, which passeth all understanding, shall keep your hearts and minds through Christ Jesus.* Philippians 4:7

Be Submissive

> *Submitting yourselves one to another in the fear of God. Wives, submit yourselves unto your own husbands, as unto the Lord. For the husband is the head of the wife, even as Christ is the head of the church: and he is the saviour of the body. Therefore as the church is subject unto Christ, so let the wives be to their own husbands in every thing.*
> Ephesians 5:21-24

Christians are to walk in daily submission, first to God, and then to each other. Are you and your partner walking in humility? Christians should heed Paul's words:

One Flesh

Let nothing be done through strife, and selfish ambition; but in lowliness of mind, while each esteem others better than ourselves. Philippians 2:3

Be Examples

Remember: marriage is symbolic of the union of Jesus Christ and His Church:

> *Husbands, love your wives, even as Christ also loved the church, and gave himself for it; that he might sanctify and cleanse it with the washing of water by the word, that he might present it to himself a glorious church, not having spot, or wrinkle, or any such thing; but that it should be holy and without blemish.* Ephesians 5:25-27

Wives are to submit themselves to their own husband. But, first, have you submitted fully to Christ as Head of your life? If you have not submitted to His headship, then, you will not be successful in submitting to a mate. God's grace enables us to walk in humility so that we are willing to submit to His delegated authority:

> *Likewise, ye younger, submit yourselves unto the elder. Yea, all of you be subject one to an-*

other, and be clothed with humility: for God resisteth the proud, and giveth grace to the humble.   1 Peter 5:5

Before you enter into a marriage covenant, it is vital that both of you be found in the Person of Jesus Christ. Having first submitted to Christ, then you have the power to become a son or daughter of God, and you can begin to grow from faith to faith and from glory to glory.

Remember what Amos said:

Can two walk together, except they be agreed?
                                                Amos 3:3

Therefore, as the church is subject unto Christ, so let the wives be to their own husbands in everything.   Ephesians 5:24

The husband is the head and savior of the wife.

As we have seen, way back in Genesis 3:16, God delegated to the husband the responsibility to rule over his wife. So, as Christ is Head of the Church, the husband is head of the wife. In marriage, the wife typifies the Church, which is the Bride of Christ. As

One Flesh

Christ is the Savior of the Church, His Bride, so the husband is to be the savior of the wife.

What is a savior? *Strong's* defines it this way: "Greek (sode'-zo) safe, to save; deliver or protect; heal, preserve, do well, be (make) whole." As Christ is to the Church, so is the husband to the wife—when his duties are carried out in love and humility. The husband protects, provides and cares for the well-being of the wife.

Paul said it again to the Corinthians:

> *But I would have you to know, the head of every man is Christ; and the head of the woman is the man; and the head of Christ is God.*
>
> 1 Corinthians 11:3

Therefore, husbands are to love their wives, even as Christ loved the church, and gave Himself for it.

If you are a husband-to-be, can you declare categorically that you are willing to give yourself for your bride-to-be? Are you willing to suffer long and cover the faults and flaws of your bride? Are you willing to pray for and pray with and make intercession for your bride? Are you willing to advocate for and to vindicate your bride? Are you willing to go countless miles for your bride? Are you willing to die for your bride, to lay down your very life for her? Are you willing to forgive your bride her faults, without keeping count of the wrongs done? Paul wrote to the Colossians:

> *Husbands, love your wives, and be not bitter against them.*   Colossians 3:19

A faithful husband must love his wife as much today as he did when he first fell in love with her, and must love her the same (until death parts them) or until the Church is caught away.

Husbands are to pray and intercede for their wives. When the husband prays for both himself and his wife, that moves God to set apart both in sanctification. Husbands are to remain steadfast in the Word of God and are always to pray as the high priest of the marriage and home. The result of doing this is sanctification through the washing of the Word. A home should always be filled with prayer, the Word and the peace of God. Therefore, every groom-to-be should be a man of prayer, steadfast in the Word, always seeking the wisdom of God.

What does it mean *to sanctify*? This word can be defined as "Greek (hag'-ee-os) sacred, physically, pure, morally blameless, or religious; (mentally) to venerate; venerate: to feel or show deep respect for (someone or something) that is considered great, holy; reverential respect, to honor."

Be Faithful to Your Heavenly Commission

So ought men to love their wives as their own bodies. He that loveth his wife loveth himself. For no man ever yet hated his own flesh; but nourisheth and cherisheth it, even as the Lord the church: for we are members of his body, of his flesh, and of his bones.

Ephesians 5:28-30

A husband is to nourish and cherish his bride as the Lord nourishes and cherishes the Church. What does it mean *to nourish*? "Greek (ek-tref'-o) to rear up to maturity, to cherish or train; bring up, to pamper." *To cherish* is "Greek (thal'-po) to warm, to brood, to foster." A husband works with God to aid and assist his wife in becoming the product God has created her to be. Because a husband loves his body, he nourishes and cherishes it. This is also exactly what he is to do for his wife.

A husband must be kind, gentle, tender and merciful toward his wife, never harsh, bitter or abusive. He must esteem and value her highly. He must reverence her and affirm her before God and others. Peter wrote:

> *Husbands are to dwell with the wives according to knowledge, giving honour unto the wife, as unto the weaker* [non-masculine] *vessel, and as being heirs together of the grace of life; that your prayers be not hindered.*　　1 Peter 3:7

Be Ready to Do Your Part

> *That he might present it to himself a glorious church, not having spot, or wrinkle, or any such thing; but that it should be holy and without blemish.*　　　　　　Ephesians 5:27

A husband should always be ready to present his wife. If you are a groom, will you work hard to present your bride before God and others? *To present* means "Greek (par-is-tay-mee), to stand beside, to exhibit, pro offer, (especially), recommend, commend, present, prove, provide, or show." In all things, the husband should be aware that his mission is to present his bride.

Just as the Church reflects Christ and His divine attributes, so the presentation of the wife represents the husband's character and qualities. The husband works together with God for a successful presentation.

Be Faithful to God's Plan

> *For this cause shall a man leave his father and mother, and shall be joined unto his wife, and they two shall be one flesh. This is a great mystery: but I speak concerning Christ and the church. Nevertheless let every one of you in particular so love his wife even as himself; and the wife see that she reverence her husband.* Ephesians 5:31-33

The two of you must show yourselves to be Spirit-filled believers and serious people ready for a life of peace and prosperity.

> *Let the peace of God rule in your hearts, to the which also ye are called in one body; and be ye thankful. Let the word of Christ dwell in you richly in all wisdom; teaching and admonishing one another in psalms and hymns and spiritual songs, signing with grace in your hearts to the Lord. And whatsoever ye do in word or deed, do all in the name of the*

Living in Harmony

Lord Jesus, giving thanks to God and the Father by him.   Colossians 3:15-17

Study Questions

1. What does living in harmony mean to you?

2. What are you willing to sacrifice to live in harmony with your spouse?

3. At what point would you refuse to sacrifice just to live in harmony?

4. Do you believe that a sacrifice is an unselfish act of love?

5. Do you believe that you and your spouse praying together would help you to live in harmony?

6. Is there evidence of the fruit of the Spirit in you and/or your partner?

7. Do you understand the allegory Jesus used for marriage, that of Christ and His Bride, the Church?

8. Study Ephesians 4:26. What does it mean to you?

9. Is getting angry a sin? Explain your answer.

10. The best antidote for anger is forgiveness. Are you willing to forgive your spouse and wipe the slate clean every time?

CHAPTER 11

Not Bringing Your Past with You

Therefore if any man be in Christ, he is a new creature: old things are passed away; behold, all things are become new. 2 Corinthians 5:17

I encourage every one of you to affirm your relationship with Christ before you commit to a lifelong relationship with another person. A genuine relationship with Christ will be manifested in your life by the fruit you are bearing. Evidence of such fruits will be: *agape* love, holiness, joy, purity, humility, peace, gentleness, goodness, faith, patience, gratitude, etc. Are these fruits evident in your life and in the life of your partner? I would that both of you would take a self-inventory and that this inventory be both moral and spiritual. Be sure that both of you

One Flesh

have confessed Christ and are making every effort to live for Him.

Honesty before God and with yourself will prove to be the best practice. Marriage is a covenant between a man and a woman. It requires taking a vow before God and other witnesses. When God instituted the first marriage, He laid down the rules He expected men to follow. Unfortunately, today, marriage vows are taken very lightly. At the first misunderstanding, if there is no resolution, the next step is too often divorce. But marriage is a serious covenant that should not be broken except under certain rare circumstances outlined in the Bible.

Marriage is a serious full-time job, and there is no room in it for baggage from the past. Some of us refuse to face the content of luggage labeled THE PAST, and yet we don't seem to mind dragging it around with us everywhere we go. I call it "the dirty laundry."

This bag is filled with emotional struggles, damaged goods, unresolved issues, anger, bitterness, unforgiveness, abandonment, guilt, betrayal, resentment, etc. This dirty laundry bag gives off a foul odor, and it contaminates everything it touches:

There is nothing from without a man that entering into him can defile him: but the things which come out of him, those are they that defile the man.   Mark 7:15-23

Keep thy heart with all diligence; for out of it are the issues of life.   Proverbs 4:23

The heart contains life's issues, and if those issues are left unresolved, it could prove disastous to your marriage and other relationships. See to it that such past issues are faced and resolved before entering into a covenant with another person.

Both the man and the woman must seek godly counsel, and a credible deliverance minister to aid in dealing with any unresolved issues of the past. It is vital to address and work through these issues and to have deliverance administered before committing to another relationship. If you fail to allow God and time to heal your hurts, your next relationship will suffer because of it.

Jesus met a woman who was bowed over with heavy burdens:

And, behold, there was a woman which had a spirit of infirmity eighteen years, and was bowed together, and could in no wise raise up

One Flesh

herself. And when Jesus saw her, he called her to him, and said unto her, Woman, thou art loosed from thine infirmity, and he laid his hands on her; and immediately she was made straight, and glorified God. Luke 13:11-13

This woman had carried a lot of stuff around with her for far too long, and the weight of it all had eventually afflicted her—spiritually, mentally and physically. For eighteen years, this woman of faith, a daughter of Abraham, had been bound by Satan. And, just like this woman, some of us, yes, even Church members, are bound. We act as if we have it all together, but Jesus sees it all. He knows it all, and He is calling us to stand upright in liberty and truth. Jesus wants to set each of us free and loose us from our past.

Satan's goal is to keep all of God's people in bondage, but Jesus came that we might have an abundant life. Through Christ, we can live free from vengeance, wrath, anger, malice, resentment, hatred, envy and all the rest. We are required to forgive and let go of our anger, so that we can be forgiven and God can continue to bless us.

We all have a past. If you believe there is something in your past that is presently affecting you, this should be resolved before entering a new union. If, for some reason, this is not possible, it should be discussed with your partner. Do not be deceived. If this matter goes unreported and unresolved, it may well destroy your marriage. Coverups, as is their nature, will always eventually blow up.

Study Questions

1. Have you experienced conflicts lately? If so, did you take care to get them resolved? If not, why not?

2. In your past relationships, did you come away with unresolved issues? If so, name them and the other party involved. What steps are you currently taking to get those issues resolved?

3. How were they resolved?

4. Have you experienced rejection in your past? If so, how was it resolved?

5. Were you betrayed before? If so, how did you handle the betrayal?

6. Are you still angry? If so, why?

CHAPTER 12

Forgetting What Is Past

Brethren, I count not myself to have apprehended: but this one thing I do, forgetting those things which are behind and reaching forth unto those things which are before, I press toward the mark for the prize of the high calling of God in Christ Jesus. Philippians 3:13-14

Like anyone else, Christians have past hurts that must be forgiven and forgotten. The demon of "memory recall" must be cast out, for this is a demon whose expertise is to keep alive the memory of past wrongs and failures. Memory recall is like a CD that is set to replay over and over again. It keeps alive all past hurts, pains, and failures.

Jesus had a strange encounter with a man known as the Gadarene:

One Flesh

And they came over unto the other side of the sea, into the country of the Gadarenes. And when he was come out of the ship, immediately there met him out of the tombs a man with an unclean spirit, who had his dwelling among the tombs; and no man could bind him, no, not with chains: because that he had been often bound with fetters and chains, and the chains had been plucked asunder by him, and the fetters broken in pieces: neither could any man tame him. And always, night and day, he was in the mountains, and in the tombs, crying, and cutting himself with stones. Mark 5:1-5

This poor man was possessed with a legion of demons, and part of the result was that he made his dwelling among the tombs. What does this mean to us today? *Tombs* "Greek, (mnay-mi'-on) *mnemeion*; a remembrance, (place of interment): grave, sepulcher, tomb." In other words, he lived among old and terrible memories.

Before you commit to marriage, you must leave the tomb of your past. Getting married in such a condition would be a deliberate act of dishonesty and deception, both to yourself and to your partner.

Forgetting What Is Past

This is another reason to rid yourself of the "dirty laundry bag" of the past.

In the case of the Gadarene, there were legions of demons tormenting him, and there may be many demons following you too because you have refused to face the past and deal with it once and for all. When you decide to deal with your past, you are taking back your freedom.

As terrible as this man's condition was, a simple command from Jesus set him free, and you can be free too.

The apostle Paul was determined to forget his past. He said:

> But this one thing I do, forgetting those things which are behind and reaching forth unto those things which are before, I press toward the mark for the prize of the high calling of God in Christ Jesus.   Philippians 3:13-14

You may have heard someone say, "I forgive [him or her], but I can never forget." That statement alone lets us know that this individual has not yet learned what it is to be in Christ. Christ forgave us our trespasses (which were many), and yet in all His righteousness, He says to us today:

One Flesh

This is the covenant that I will make with them after those days, saith the Lord, I will put my laws into their hearts and in their minds will I write them; and their sins and iniquities will I remember no more. Hebrews 10:16-17

As far as the east is from the west, so far hath he removed our transgressions from us.
Psalm 103:12

If God has forgotten the past, that is an example for us to follow.

Study Questions

1. How frequently do you find yourself discussing a past occurrence which has caused you pain?

2. Why do you think you continue to relive this particular incident?

3. What are the means by which you have tried to help work through this pain?

At this point, I again recommend my book, *Breaking Free*.[1] This book is structured to help guide you through to healing and deliverance from negative emotions like unforgiveness.

---

1. (Greenwell Springs, Louisiana, McDougal & Associates: 2019)

CHAPTER 13

Avoiding Controlling Behaviors

For jealousy is the rage of a man: therefore, he will not spare in the day of vengeance.

Proverbs 6:34

Jealousy is cruel as the grave.

Song of Solomon 8:6b

In this section, we will use the terms, *jealousy*, *jealous* and *controlling* interchangeably. For the sake of clarity, these terms must be used repeatedly in identifying these destructive behaviors. It's important to inform the reader that these behaviors will be evident in both the jealous and controlling individual.

What is *jealousy*? It is "the state or feeling of being jealous." *Jealous* is an adjective that means "feeling or showing envy of someone or their achievements and advantages. 2. feeling or showing suspicion of someone's unfaithfulness in a relationship. Ex. "a jealous boyfriend" suspicious- distrustful- mistrustful- doubting- insecure- anxious- apprehensive of rivals- possessive- proprietorial- overprotective- clinging- controlling- dominating."

What we have come to call "controlling" is a type of possessive behavior that is demonstrated sometimes in selfishness, pride, aggressiveness and dominance and exhibited in an unloving manner. There is a normal limit to control that is utilized to maintain order or safety, and anything more than this is considered possessive or worse.

You might think it is flattering or even amusing when the person you are planning to spend the rest of your life with seems controlling and possessive. You might even feel super special that he or she would care so much about you. But do not be deceived. A controlling person is a possessive person. If left untreated, this person will destroy every relationship they touch. These behaviors are not healthy ones and should never be ignored.

Married people will share most everything, but each person also needs a certain privacy, and that must be the boundary. It is normal and healthy for each individual to have relationships, and to respect each other's privacy. A healthy relationship is originated and nurtured from having healthy boundaries. When one encroaches on the other's privacy, it becomes a violation.

An intrusion violates boundaries and leaves an opening for the enemy to enter, bringing with him distrust, suspicions, and doubt. If this broken edge is not mended quickly, it will allow the strongman of jealousy to enter the relationship. Always respect the other person's boundaries. Remember, you are one flesh, but two distinct and individual souls. Trust starts with respect for the other person.

In the beginning, God said the two would become one flesh. But, although they are one flesh, they are still individuals who each possesses a soul. Each has an identity that continues to develop throughout their lives. Even after marriage, the two, with the aid of their mate, will continue to grow and develop into the person God intended them to be. Jealousy on the part of either mate will impede the growth of both individuals. It will cripple their relationship and will sabotage the marriage. Jealousy is a personal issue (spiritual stronghold) that needs to be resolved before committing to others.

The person operating under the control of jealousy is not a well person. This person will plant an idea in his head (imagination), and nothing will change that idea. He or she sees what he or she sees, regardless of the truth. Jealous people do not trust anyone, and they cannot be trusted, because their mind is sick, and their thoughts are sick. Jealousy does not respect boundaries, nor is it concerned about one's privacy.

If your dream partner is showing signs of jealousy, this is a red flag that should not be ignored. Love tends to blind us to truth, yet it doesn't deny truth. Stop, pray much, and wait on God before you make a more serious commitment.

Avoiding the Jezebel Spirit

King Solomon had a lot to say about the spirit of pride in his proverbs. Pride will set you up, and pride will take you down. The prideful spirit is a spirit of destruction. The wife of King Ahab, Queen Jezebel by name, was a perfect picture of a prideful spirit. Although no one wants to be told that a spirit of Jezebel is operating in their lives, this spirit is real and is adamantly opposing our homes, churches, and communities.

When talking about the Jezebel spirit, because we associate it with Queen Jezebel, we identify it with the female gender. But the Jezebel spirit has no gender. This spirit works through men as well as women. Both males and females are targets of Jezebel's plan to cause destruction, and Jezebel's source is always Satan.

Some people are aware of a Jezebel spirit operating in them, and they believe that it is "no big deal," that God knows their heart so He will excuse it. Then we have others who out of ignorance allow Jezebel to operate in their lives. So, let's expose some of Jezebel's character traits.

Jezebel is controlling, domineering and aggressive, has no respect for authority, is loud and two-faced, is a slanderer with the tongue, a murderer, a liar, a manipulator and an intimidator, is overbearing, self-centered, stubborn, self-willed, disobedient and prideful. Jezebel hates repentance, humility and obedience (see 1 Kings 16-31).

Study Questions

1. Do you believe that controlling someone signifies love?

2. Do you think it is right for someone to check your telephone logs, emails and SMSs?

3. When someone controls you, do you think they trust you?

4. Is there comfort in a controlling or possessive relationship?

5. How do you feel about someone choosing your friends or even if you are allowed to have friends?

6. Are you or your partner controlling and possessive? If so, how do you think the marriage will end?

CHAPTER 14

Learning to Express Love

It [love] is not rude; it is not self-seeking, it is not provoked [nor overly sensitive and easily angered]; it does not take into account a wrong endured. It does not rejoice at injustice, but rejoices with the truth [when right and truth prevail]. Love bears all things [regardless of what comes], believes all things [looking for the best in each one], hopes all things [remaining steadfast during difficult times], endures all things [without weakening]. Love never fails [it never fades nor ends]. But as for prophecies, they will pass away; as for tongues, they will cease; as for the gift of special knowledge, it will pass away.

1 Corinthians 13:5-8, AMP

The apostle Paul gave us great insights into the meaning of love. He told us what love does and what love does not. We might call it a demonstration of love.

A Demonstration of Love

- Love is not rude.
- Love is not self-seeking.
- Love is not easily provoked [nor overly sensitive and easily angered].
- Love does not dictate, nor does it dominate others.
- Love does not take into account a wrong endured.
- Love does not rejoice at injustice, but rejoices with the truth [when right and truth prevail].
- Love bears all things [regardless of what comes],
- Love believes all things [looking for the best in each one],
- Love hopes all things [remaining steadfast during difficult times],
- Love endures all things [without weakening].
- Love never fails [it never fades nor ends].

Learning to Express Love

Love is patient and kind. It treats me tenderly and talks to me softly. Love is not envious, jealous, possessive, distrustful, or greedy. Love releases me and sets me free. Love does not brag, boast, flaunt itself or get puffed up. It does not behave itself unseemly. Love is never rude, ill mannered or disrespectful. It does not seek its own, is not selfish, self-centered, "me" minded or self-seeking.

Love is not easily provoked, not easily angered, and keeps no record of wrongdoing. It easily and quickly forgets offenses.

Love thinks no evil. It has no payback list, no record of wrongs. It does not rejoice in iniquity, but rejoices in the truth. It bears all things, putting up with and overlooking mistakes. It believes all things. It hopes all things. It endures all things.

Real love stays in love. It never fails. It remains and holds things together.

Oh, that this simplicity of love would be more visible in our world today. Currently, the United States is ranked number ten among the nations with the highest divorce rates in the world and is also showing a declining rate in marriages. Every six seconds an American marriage will end in divorce. Fifty-three percent of all marriages are failing.

As a result, many are waiting longer to get married. Those who are already married find it so easy to split up, declare the marriage over, sign a paper and go their way. If no children are involved, divorce is so easy these days. Some states make it more difficult than others, but in most, it is far too easy.

The ten most common reasons given for divorce today are:

1. Infidelity
2. Money Issues
3. Lack of communication
4. Constant arguing
5. Weight gain
6. Unrealistic expectations
7. Lack of intimacy
8. Lack of equality
9. Not being prepared for marriage
10. Abuse[8]

According to Dr. Mensa Otabil and his teaching "Commitment Is the Foundation of a Lasting and Successful Marriage,"[9] the lack of commitment is the main reason for divorce and one of the top three at

8. https://www.marriage.com/advice/divorce/10-most-common-reasons-for-divorce/
9. From a message on YOU TUBE, accessed on March 3, 2019

seventy-five percent. His definition of commitment is "the act of giving yourself wholly to another."[10] People who are selfish, self-centered or are narcissistic, therefore, cannot have any meaningful relationships.

Ruth 1:15-18 shows us five kinds of commitment:

1. Personal commitment
2. Where you are found, I will commit.
3. Wherever you go, I will go.
4. I will belong to what you belong to.
5. Your God shall be my God.

Where you go, I will go.   Verse 16, AMP

In other words, wherever your journey, I will go with you—no matter the changes required.

Your people will be my people, and your God, my God.   Verse 16, AMP

When you take vows before God and others, you have made those same commitments. Ruth was telling Naomi, "I am committed to you." When we marry a partner, we have commitments to them that must be fulfilled. *"Your people shall be my people"* is one com-

10. Ibid

mitment that is so easily shunned and left out of the preparatory stages of marriage. It is vital to get to know your partner and their family because, like it or not, they will all become *your* family. When you marry someone, you literally marry their whole family.

Your god shall be my god.   Verse 16, AMP

Again, it is very important to know the god your partner is serving. This god must be identified, as well as its doctrine and its service. As we have seen, two cannot walk together except they be agreed.

Naomi served the God of Israel, but Ruth was a Moabite. Ruth had to choose between her god and the God of Naomi, for it is impossible to serve two gods at once.

Ruth was saying, "Where you go, I will follow." She was committed to Naomi, regardless of where life's journey would lead her. Despite the twists and turns, the mountains and valleys, the wildernesses and desert places. She was saying, "There will be changes along the way, but I am with you regardless of those changes." That is real commitment.

You must commit to the person you desire to marry, commitment to who and what that person is at the time. Never go into a marriage with the notion: "they will change." Be committed to who and what you are planning to spend the rest of your life with or it may affect the long-term success of your marriage.

Be committed to your marriage and be willing to work to make the marriage successful. You must give what you think is impossible to give.

Stay committed by respecting your partner. Respect will go further than your initial feelings of love. Respect is the foundation of marriage. Respect will survive when all else is lost.

If your partner doesn't respect you now, do not marry that person. It's that simple. If the person is insulting and disgraces you, do not marry that person. It's that simple.

Respecting people comes long before they earn it. Someone who doesn't show you respect is still immature. Therefore, they cannot show respect. Growth is natural, but maturity is optional. Marrying an immature person is just asking for trouble.

Commit to your marriage with an institutional forgiveness. Be ready to forgive, even seventy times seven:

Jesus saith unto him, I say not unto thee, Until seven times: but, Until seventy times seven.
                                    Matthew 18:22

One Flesh

Commit to your spousal duties. Commit to your marriage with a sacrifice. A sacrifice is often with blood. You may not have to die physically, but you must die to self and to your own desires; and you must do it for the sake of someone else.

Yes, marriage is just that serious. Don't enter into it lightly. This is the reason for the traditional opening to the Christian marriage ceremony:

> *Dearly beloved, we are gathered here today to witness the union of (Groom's Name) and (Bride's Name) in holy matrimony, which is an honorable estate, that is not to be entered into unadvisedly or lightly, but reverently and soberly.*

Are you serious about your upcoming wedding? God is. He wishes you well and has made every provision for you to have a happy and prosperous life. Take advantage of it. Don't squander your opportunity by your own foolishness.

Study Questions

1. Are you ready for a lifetime commitment?

2. Do you love God and yourself?

3. Do you expect your partner to make you whole? If so, how?

4. How do you show love?

5. How much of yourself are you willing to give to make your marriage work?

6. If you must give more than you bargained for, how will you commit to the marriage?

7. Are you willing to forgive your spouse every day of your married life?

8. Do you and your partner have respect for each other?

9. Do you have healthy boundaries in the relationship right now? If not, why not?

10. If there are children involved, you must love those children now and forever. Are you ready to share your spouse with them?

A Prayer for You

Father, thank You for preparing me for my compatible mate. Thank You for being my example of love and commitment. You are Lord over my life. In You, we live and move and have our being, as certain also of Your own poets have said, for we are also Your children. I know whom I have believed and am persuaded that You, Father, are able to keep that which I have committed unto You.

I am no longer a child and yet I need Your guidance. Show me Your ways, O Lord; teach me Your paths. I will stand upon Your Words and continue in them because Your Word is a lamp unto my feet and a light unto my path. Light up my path and show me the way and I will walk therein. You said, "It is not good that man should be alone; I will make him an help meet."

One Flesh

Thank You for designing that special mate just for me. Let us be found in You, O Lord. Bless our union, and bless our children. Give us Your wisdom and let this union model Christ and His Bride, the Church. Help us to build our home and make that home a house of prayer. Help us to work together in unity, for You delight in oneness. May Your love abound in our hearts yet more and more in knowledge and in all wisdom. Father, make us to increase and abound in love one toward another and toward all men, even as we do toward You.

I pray this in Jesus' mighty name, Amen![1]

---

1. For additional study on the essence of this prayer, see Acts 17:28, Psalms 25:4, 119:15 and 133:1-3, Genesis 2:18, Philippians 1:9 and 1 Thessalonians 3:12

Resources

1. The King James Study Bible (Nashville, TN, Thomas Nelson Publishers: 1988)
2. *Overcoming Rejection* by Frank Hammond (Kirkwood, MO, Impact Christian Books: 2014)
3. https://www.marriage.com/advice/divorce/10-most-common-reasons-for-divorce/
4. Otabil, Dr. Mensa, "Commitment Is the Foundation of a Lasting and Successful Marriage" a message viewed on YOU TUBE on March 3, 2019.
5. *Boundaries* by Henry Cloud and John Townsend (Grand Rapids, MI, Zondervan: 2002)

Author Contact Page

Jane P. McCoy
Broken Wings Healing Ministries International
P.O. Box 366
Carencro, Louisiana 70520

Phone: 337-356-1583

www.janeministries.org

Jane Ministries on Facebook @janeministries
Personal Facebook ID: Jane McCoy

Books by Jane P. McCoy

Breaking Free

A Manual for Finding Deliverance through Prayer and Fasting

Jane P. McCoy

One Flesh

Updated Edition

Discovering Kingdom Principles for Your Marriage

Jane P. McCoy

Unmasking the Roaring Lion

Understanding Fear and Its Design

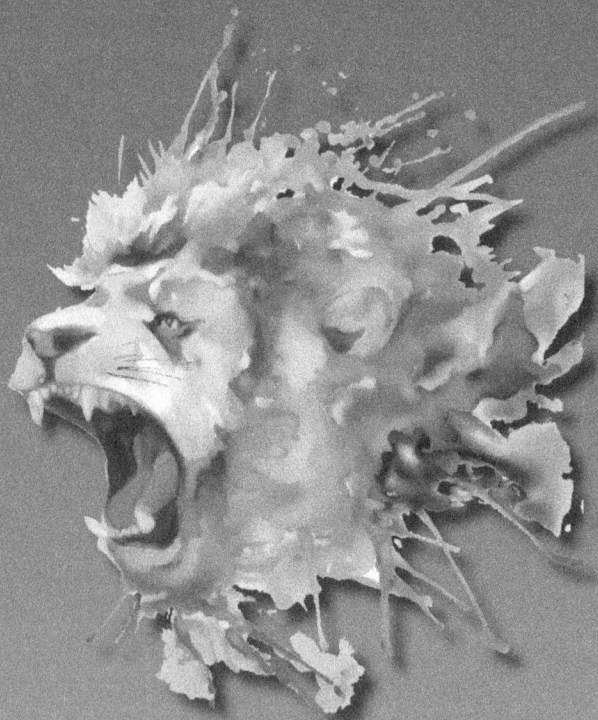

Jane P. McCoy

SOUL TIES
An Inside Look

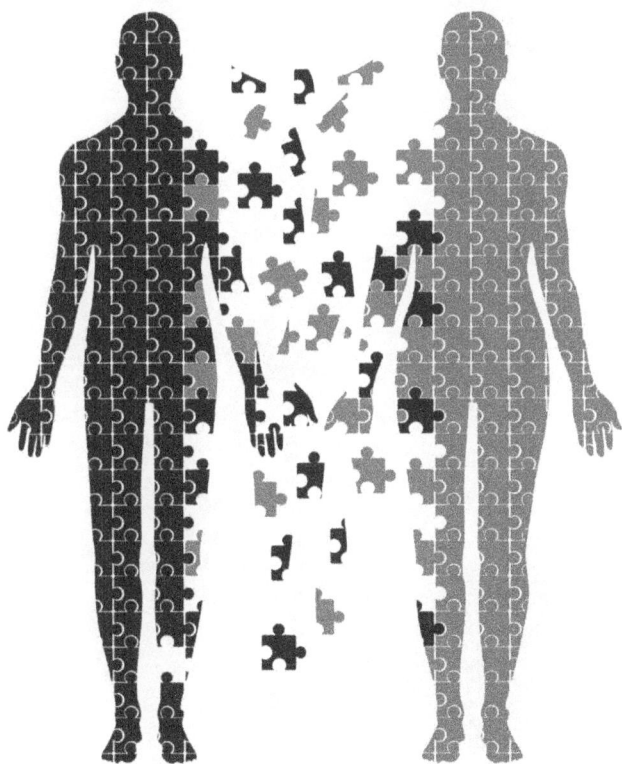

Jane P. McCoy

www.ingramcontent.com/pod-product-compliance
Lightning Source LLC
LaVergne TN
LVHW011331080426
835513LV00006B/289